Alan Bauer is committed to *rightly handling the word of truth.* In his Biblical exegesis, Alan seeks to let the Bible to speak for itself... which unfortunately is not how all teachers and preachers approach Biblical exposition. As a teacher, Alan is able to bring out meaningful observations straight from the text that are often overlooked by the average Bible reader. He encourages his students and/or audience to not only observe what the text explicitly says, but how to process through the implications of the text in such a way that brings deeper meaning and understanding to the Bible student. He also encourages his audience to challenge some of the more "mainstream" interpretations of certain Biblical texts that are not grounded on what the text actually says. Alan will often engage his audience by presenting them with a "mainstream" view of a given text where the associated interpretation has failed to take into consideration several key factors in the text. He then has them to carefully observe the details of that text for themselves in order for them to discover details or facts that may have been overlooked by the "mainstream" interpretation. Additionally, Alan assists his students in identifying an alternative interpretation that is sometimes contrary to the mainstream view but is based strictly on the Biblical facts in the text. Alan clearly desires to help Bible readers to examine Scriptural texts more thoughtfully and carefully, allowing them the best opportunity to accurately interpret the meaning of Scripture.

Although most of Alan's exegetical methods are the same as those commonly used by most scholarly Bible interpreters, his self-developed C.L.A.P. method of interpretation can be used by Biblical teachers and beginning Bible readers alike. While beginning Bible readers will appreciate the C.L.A.P. method for the framework it provides, Bible teachers should find that this methodology enhances their previous understanding of the Biblical text. Whether a person is reading through the Bible devotionally for themselves or preparing to present the Word of God to others, Alan's C.L.A.P. method is an invaluable tool when it comes to *how to see.*

—JEREMY DICKSON PASTOR OF FREEDOM CHURCH, BALTIMORE

HOW TO SEE: READING GOD'S WORD WITH NEW EYES

A · D · BAUER

SQUARE HALO BOOKS

In Christian art, the square halo identified a living person presumed to be a saint. Square Halo Books is devoted to publishing works that present contextually sensitive biblical studies, and practical instruction consistent with the Doctrines of the Reformation. The goal of Square Halo Books is to provide materials useful for encouraging and equipping the saints.

©2022 Square Halo Books, Inc.
P.O. Box 18954
Baltimore, MD 21206
www.SquareHaloBooks.com

All Scripture quotations, unless otherwise indicated, are taken from the Holy Bible, New Revised Standard Version.

ISBN 978-1-941106-25-9
Library of Congress Control Number: 2022941216

All rights reserved. No part of this book may be reproduced without permission from the publisher, except by a reviewer who may quote brief passages in a review; nor may any part of this book be reproduced, stored in a retrieval system or transmitted in any form by any means (electronic, mechanical, photocopying, recorded or other), without permission from the publisher.

Printed in the United States of America

This book is dedicated
to Diana DiPasquale.

*For years, she encouraged me to be fearless as I saw
with new eyes unexpected things in the Scriptures.
Together we have explored the meaning and applications of
different passages in God's Word. Her reward was to drag me
all over the globe where we witnessed the majesty of God's
creation in nature and through works of art where beauty
reflects the divine Creator. Diana has taught me
to appreciate art and poetry (in spite of my credentials
as a cultural barbarian). I love you Diana.*

CONTENTS

00	INTRODUCTION	09
01	WHY WE NEED TO INTERPRET SCRIPTURE	13
02	PRACTICAL RULES	29
03	THE CLAP METHOD	37
04	PATTERNS IN SCRIPTURE	55
05	OTHER HELPFUL RULES	61
06	INTERPRETING GENESIS 1—3	67
07	INTERPRETING REVELATION	85
08	HARMONIZING PASSAGES	107
09	TRANSLATIONS AND OTHER STUDY TOOLS	121

00

INTRODUCTION

We have read the Word of God. We think we know it all, but we are sometimes as blind as we can be. I have to say "we" here because I am no more immune to this blindness than anyone else. If we are familiar with the Bible and come to it expecting that it won't tell us anything new, rereading the same things over and over again can seem tedious. But God's Word is filled with details we often overlook because they seem to differ from the version of the story that we have always known. This is true not only in obscure passages in the minor prophets. We miss things in the creation narrative. We miss things in accounts of the birth of Jesus. We miss things in the classic Bible stories, like those of David and Samson, that many of us have heard since our youth.

How is it possible that we miss things in the biblical text that we have read repeatedly? That is really the question, isn't it? Rather than seeing Scripture objectively, we put a filter between us and the Word of God. This can happen in a number of ways.

Since we are sure we already know the stories, we may rely on something other than a careful reading of the biblical text. We may find it easier to accept a lesson we were taught in Sunday school or church than to expend the effort to look at the text for ourselves. In the same way, we may depend on our memory of what we read instead of rereading the passage. We cannot see what we miss if we do not actually read the Scriptures ourselves.

Another way we filter the text is by relying on our theological training and systematic theology framework to tell us what the text says. No one, on this side of eternity, has perfect theology. We may know all the supporting passages for our views, but if we allow our theology to determine what a biblical passage says, we can miss what is in the text. God's Word must determine our theology; our theology must not determine what we see in God's Word.

We apply another sort of filter when we decide what is acceptable for God to say in His Word. A brilliant pastor once said, "We're all about the Word until our experience contradicts it. Then we are all about the experience." If we don't like what a passage says, or if we don't agree with it, we fix it. We may try to explain away the troublesome passage, or we may just disregard what the Bible says.

These various filters block us from seeing what is in the Bible. Sadly, we often don't even know that we have these filters in place. Have you ever been outside when the weather gradually clouded up and you only realized later that you were wearing sunglasses? Until you noticed the glasses and took them off, it seemed unusually dark outside. Reading the Bible with these filters in place can make the text seem dim and cloudy.

I hope we all read books that provide tools that help us interpret the Bible. These tools give us the ability to read the Bible in a way that allows us to understand the meaning of the text. What this book will attempt to do is take you beyond those tools, to a new set of tools that deal with our self-imposed blindness. In some ways this is like comparing an automotive manual, that tells you everything about your car, to taking a test ride. You only learn the feel of the brakes, how the car takes turns, and the positioning of the seat by actually driving the car. In the same way, you may know all the rules about interpreting Scripture, but you still may not see things clearly because no one has put you in the driver's seat and shown you the kinds of things we all miss.

00: INTRODUCTION

In this book, I will provide examples of areas where we have failed to see things that are obvious in the text. Some of these you will likely find easy to accept. Others will be more challenging, because they deal with passages that we firmly believe we already understand. We may have used these passages to support a particular theological view, which makes it even harder to acknowledge that our established interpretation was incorrect. But I want to encourage you to try to get beyond what you have always known. I hope you can revisit these passages with new eyes and read the biblical text objectively.

I will also try to offer explanations of how the new interpretation is helpful to our theology, faith, and practice. We may not always know what difference a new interpretation makes. I can only say that if we are interpreting the Scriptures correctly, at some point we may find the reason it makes a difference. I teach theology. There have been a number of times that my wife, who is a biblical counselor, has shown me practical and counseling implications for passages where I had observed a new interpretation. I knew what the text said, but I needed help figuring out what the impact of that new interpretation was in the Scriptures. I should note that I am not suggesting that I see everything that is in the text. We But let's explore the Bible using this new set of tools and see if we find that the Bible, far from being filled with what we have always known, is actually interesting, exciting, and filled with new insights.

01

WHY WE NEED TO INTERPRET SCRIPTURE

Many years ago, I went with my father to an evening church service at a Baptist church. The pastor was preaching on Daniel and the abomination that causes desolation. At one point the preacher reached a climax and pointed out to the congregation that Daniel prophesied an attack using an atomic bomb. This created quite a stir, since this was something most people had not observed in this text. It was clear he had a new and powerful insight. The speaker went on to prove his point by using the very words of the text where Daniel referred to the abomination that causes desolation. He observed that Daniel's prophecy clearly says there will be an "A Bomb a Nation."

If we consider this speaker's interpretive system, we see a number of reasons he missed his goal.

- The interpretation was linguistically flawed. He took a translation from Hebrew, broke the one English word into pieces that sounded like other English words, and concluded that the real meaning of the text was the resulting English words, which described modern weapons that had nothing to do with the originally translated English word or the Hebrew word in the original text.

- The interpretation was culturally conditioned. Prophecy is often misused to support a particular view that would not have been the intent of the prophet. This leads to biblical interpretations that change as culture and technology change. We will discuss this later in the book.
- The interpretation stemmed from a preexisting theological view. Too often people come to the biblical text with their minds made up, which leads to a number of problems. We may miss things the text clearly says, because they are different than what we believe. Or we may allow teaching of almost anything that supports our position, even if that teaching disagrees with the text. We can also be blinded to the strengths of biblical positions that differ from our own.

I hope, as we proceed through this book, that we will develop skills that allow us to critique bad interpretive approaches and learn how to properly interpret the biblical text.

We will begin with a brief overview of some of the tools for interpretation that are presented in other hermeneutics books.

EXEGESIS AND APPLICATION

Exegesis involves digging into the text in a way that attempts to capture what the biblical author intended when writing the words. This is a helpful practice: getting the meaning directly from the text helps us understand what the text says.. But suppose a pastor preaches a sermon where he clearly lays out how the text is to be understood within the passage and then says "Amen" and ends his sermon. The church can be dry and dusty if it is entirely devoted to knowing things in the absence of any other interaction.

In contrast, we have probably all heard application-based teaching and preaching. This approach can lead to nonsense as the speaker says whatever he wants, often reflecting the current culture, without grounding it in the biblical text.

01: WHY WE NEED TO INTERPRET SCRIPTURE

A balanced approach helps us apply what the text means to us in our modern context, in light of what it meant to the church at the time it was written. Probably the most difficult thing for a pastor to do (and also for laypeople to do in their personal Bible study) is to take the meaning of the text, relate it to our own lives and culture, and determine what the Word of God calls us to do as a result.

WHAT WOULD WE GAIN IF WE WERE ABLE TO UNDERSTAND THE SCRIPTURES WELL AND APPLY THEM TO OUR LIVES?

Some people think that if we simply read the Bible, the meaning will almost always be clear. We have heard the saying, "God said it, I believe it, and that settles it." But to be accurate, that saying needs to be revised. It should say, "God said it, I believe what I have concluded it means—based on my presuppositions and all that I think I know, and in spite of what I don't know—and that settles it." Of course, if our presuppositions are wrong—or there are significant things we think we know that are wrong, or relevant things we don't know—our beliefs should not be settled.

Surprisingly, some take an "I believe it" approach to Revelation, which is a difficult book to interpret. Those who take that view often also hold assumptions that a particular end times view is correct and all others are wrong. But even in the biblical books that aren't dominated by imagery, what some think is clear, faces disagreement from others who think a different meaning is clear. There is a reason some are Baptists and others baptize babies. The list of disagreements in theological views is so long it is impossible to summarize them. Different views have led to the formation of many denominations. Within denominations there are groups and individuals that disagree with each other. In the US alone there are thousands of independent churches who have their own distinctives. From the many ways Christians divide themselves, we get a sense of how differently many passages can be interpreted.

SCRIPTURE INTERPRETS SCRIPTURE

With so many disagreements, is there a best approach to interpreting the Bible that should work for everyone? I believe there is, but this approach requires us to consider a number of factors and apply a number of principles.

We must start with a "Scripture interprets Scripture" approach, which holds that no passage of Scripture can be interpreted in a way that would cause it to disagree with another part of Scripture.

Using a Scripture interprets Scripture principle is helpful in a number of ways. Sometimes a more obscure passage can be clarified by reading a similar passage that is clearer. A passage is often given greater impact when it is used in another part of Scripture. So, we might read Psalm 14:1–3 and Psalm 53:1–3 and think that the statement "there is none who does good" applies only to the fool who says there is no God. But in Romans 3, Paul clarifies that we all, Jews and Gentiles alike, are under sin and none of us does good.

But a Scripture interprets Scripture approach can also be misused. If we look at Galatians 2:14, we see Paul confronting Peter.

> When I saw that they were not acting in line with the truth of the gospel, I said to Cephas in front of them all, "You are a Jew, yet you live like a Gentile and not like a Jew. How is it, then, that you force Gentiles to follow Jewish customs?"

Suppose we take the statement "You are a Jew" and, using a Scripture interprets Scripture approach, connect it to Romans 2:28–29, as one of my students once did.

> A person is not a Jew who is one only outwardly, nor is circumcision merely outward and physical. No, a person is a Jew who is one inwardly; and circumcision is circumcision of the heart, by the Spirit, not by the written code. Such a person's praise is not from other people, but from God.

01: WHY WE NEED TO INTERPRET SCRIPTURE

We end up with an interpretation that suggests that when Paul referred to Jews, he was referring to all believers, rather than to a specific conflict between Jewish and Gentile believers. If this is the case, Paul seems to be rebuking Peter, a Jew (believer), for living like a Gentile (unbeliever) and for forcing Gentiles (unbelievers) to follow Jewish customs. This interpretation can only occur when we ignore the context of the Galatians passage.

> When Cephas came to Antioch, I opposed him to his face, because he stood condemned. For before certain men came from James, he used to eat with the *Gentiles*. But when they arrived, he began to draw back and separate himself from the *Gentiles* because he was afraid of those who belonged to the circumcision group. The other *Jews* joined him in his hypocrisy, so that by their hypocrisy even Barnabas was led astray. (Galatians 2:11–13, *emphasis added*)

The context is that Peter was eating with believing Gentiles but stopped when Jewish believers from Jerusalem showed up. This passage never uses the term Jew to describe a true believer. Rather, it deals with how the church struggled to bring racial and religious Jewish believers together with Gentile believers in a single church that loved Jesus.

A Scripture interprets Scripture approach is about more than finding the same word or words used in different passages. It requires the student of the Bible to look for common meanings in separate passages that may or may not share similar words. That shared content allows one passage to help interpret another passage.

In a simple reading, many verses could appear to disagree with each other. Let's consider an example.

> In the same way, faith by itself, if it is not accompanied by action, is dead. (James 2:17)
> For we maintain that a person is justified by faith apart from the works of the law. (Romans 3:28)

HOW TO SEE: READING GOD'S WORD WITH NEW EYES

HOW SHOULD WE HANDLE THE INTERPRETATION OF TWO PASSAGES WHEN THEY DO NOT APPEAR TO SAY THE SAME THING? WHICH ONE IS RIGHT?

Using the Scripture interprets Scripture approach, we immediately reject the question of which one is right, because they are both right. We then go on to ask, how are they both right?

The passage from James must be read in context.

What good is it, my brothers and sisters, if someone claims to have *faith but has no deeds*? Can such faith save them? Suppose a brother or a sister is without clothes and daily food. If one of you says to them, "Go in peace; keep warm and well fed," but does nothing about their physical needs, what good is it? *In the same way, faith by itself, if it is not accompanied by action, is dead.*

But someone will say, "You have faith; I have deeds."

Show me your faith without deeds, and I will show you my faith by my deeds. You believe that there is one God. Good! Even the demons believe that—and shudder.

You foolish person, *do you want evidence that faith without deeds is useless?* Was not our father *Abraham* considered righteous for what he did when he offered his son Isaac on the altar? You see that *his faith and his actions were working together, and his faith was made complete by what he did.* And the scripture was fulfilled that says, "Abraham believed God, and it was credited to him as righteousness," and he was called God's friend. *You see that a person is considered righteous by what they do and not by faith alone.*

In the same way, was not even Rahab the prostitute considered righteous for what she did when she gave lodging to the spies and sent them off in a different direction? *As the body without the spirit is dead, so faith without deeds is dead.* (James 2:14–26, *emphasis added*)

01: WHY WE NEED TO INTERPRET SCRIPTURE

**FROM READING THE ENTIRE PASSAGE,
WHAT POINT IS JAMES MAKING?**

James is saying that while anyone can claim they have faith, the evidence that they truly have faith is in what they do. I can say that I can fly, but until I am actually in the air, flying about, it is an empty claim.

In contrast, Romans 3 and 4 approach the issue described in James from a completely different direction. Let's consider the context.

> What then shall we say that Abraham, our forefather according to the flesh, discovered in this matter? If, in fact, Abraham was *justified by works*, he had something to boast about—but not before God. What does Scripture say? "Abraham believed God, and it was credited to him as righteousness."
>
> Now to *the one who works, wages* are not credited as a gift but as an obligation. However, to the one who does not work but *trusts God who justifies* the ungodly, their faith is credited as righteousness. (Romans 4:1-5, *emphasis added*)

HOW DOES PAUL'S POINT DIFFER FROM THAT OF JAMES?

While James emphasizes that faith cannot exist without deeds, Paul's point is that it is faith and not deeds that make one right with God. Clearly James and Paul do not disagree. They both emphasize the place of faith, with James pointing out that the fruit a faithful person bears is proof that they have faith. We see that point also reflected in Jesus' teaching in the Gospels.

I would like to add another element to the idea of Scripture interprets Scripture. One thing many readers consistently miss is that the most mystifying parts of the Bible—imagery and apocalyptic literature—can often only be understood by conducting a Scripture interprets Scripture analysis of the imagery. This will be discussed later.

HOW TO SEE: READING GOD'S WORD WITH NEW EYES

HOW CAN WE EFFECTIVELY USE A SCRIPTURE INTERPRETS SCRIPTURE APPROACH?

To interpret Scripture with Scripture, we have to know Scripture. We have to read and study God's Word if we are to know which Scriptures to use to interpret other Scriptures. Even when we know the Scriptures, we need to pray for guidance. It is so easy to overlook words and phrases in the text that could give us greater clarity as we study a passage. If we read the Scriptures well and are devoted to knowing them, we will find gold hidden in the text.

LITERAL INTERPRETATION

To interpret the text literally we must give the text the most careful scrutiny. We need to consider the meaning of words, the passage's grammatical structure, and the genre (type) of book we are reading.

BEFORE WE GO FURTHER, WHAT PROBLEMS COULD WE CREATE BY INTERPRETING A TEXT TOO LITERALLY OR NOT LITERALLY ENOUGH?

We can miss the point of a passage if we interpret it literally but fail to recognize figures of speech and cultural practices at the time the text was written. Sometimes we miss the point being made if we interpret a text literally but out of context. This can happen when we selectively use texts that support a position we hold.

If we say we are committed to reading the biblical text literally with no need to interpret, we can easily miss how we actually impose our interpretation into the text. Doctors Fee and Stuart offer the example of Deuteronomy 22:5, which prohibits women from wearing men's clothes. Some interpreters take this literally, using it to prohibit women wearing slacks or shorts. However, when they do not follow other laws in the close context of that verse this interpretation is inconsistent.

> When you build a new house, make a parapet around your roof so that you may not bring the guilt of bloodshed on your house if some-

one falls from the roof.
  Do not plant two kinds of seed in your vineyard; if you do, not only the crops you plant but also the fruit of the vineyard will be defiled.
  Do not plow with an ox and a donkey yoked together.
  Do not wear clothes of wool and linen woven together.
Make tassels on the four corners of the cloak you wear.
(Deuteronomy 22:8-12)

If you build a new home today, will you include a parapet as instructed by this Old Testament passage? I haven't seen many people add tassels to their cloaks. It is inconsistent to interpret one verse literally while not treating the other verses in the close context the same way. We do not treat the Bible as God's Word if we use it selectively to support our preconceived notions.

When we don't interpret Scripture literally enough, we end up over-spiritualizing the text. The problem with over-spiritualizing is that imposing a non-literal meaning on the text strips God's Word of all content. I could take almost any passage, focus on some minor element in the text and, by spiritualizing it, make it say anything I want it to say. I could read about Jesus casting the demons into the pigs and, by spiritualizing the passage, speak of casting our "demons" (worries, troubles, etc.) into the "pigs" (throwing away our worthless activities) so they flee and are drowned. Or I could read about Jesus walking on water and use that passage to talk about rising above the turbulent waters of our daily struggles. Spiritualizing the text like this allows me to enrobe my own ideas in spiritual garb, lending a sort of biblical authority to whatever I want to say. This kind of spiritualizing obstructs our access to truth because it robs God's Word of its true meaning.

There is a difference between spiritualizing a text—imposing on the text whatever we choose to have it say—and applying a text. For example, David often writes in the Psalms about God destroying his enemies. Though we may not face physical enemies the way David did, we do have opponents whose actions are very real. We can appropriately apply the lesson of the Psalms to the enemies we have, and we can draw comfort from the Psalms as they speak of how God delivers His children from their enemies.

LITERARY ANALYSIS

Literary analysis is important because how we evaluate what we read in Scripture varies depending on the kind of literature we are reading. We intuitively interpret passages containing poetry differently than a Pauline epistle that presents factual theological teaching. Some parts of Scripture are wisdom teachings that may or may not contain poetry. Others are historic narratives. We can gain some idea of the genre of a book by how it is grouped with other books.

The first five books of the Bible (the Pentateuch) are considered the Law. There are many laws listed within these books, along with the penalties for breaking the laws. There are, however, parts of the Pentateuch that contain history and songs/poetry. The reader has to consider not only the type of book being read but also the content of the passage within that book.

Literary analysis is important, but it can be abused. As with any other course of study, if you come to the task with your decision already made, you will get the conclusion you desire. Those who reject the supernatural will ascribe miracle stories to the category of historical fiction. Some readers use literary analysis to argue against the historicity of particular biblical books. They argue that a particular book was never intended to record actual events but is instead a dramatic poem.

Take the example of Jonah. Even some scholars who believe the Bible to be infallible teach that the book of Jonah is non-historical. They point to the second chapter of Jonah, which is written in a poetic style, and say the entire book is a non-historical poem. They support that claim by pointing out that the king of Nineveh is not named, and that the text is generally vague about exactly when the events described occurred.

SO, HOW SHOULD WE VIEW JONAH? IS HE HISTORICAL? WHAT ARGUMENT COULD BE MADE THAT THE BOOK OF JONAH DOES INTEND TO TEACH HISTORY?

There are some major concerns about viewing Jonah as a non-historic poem. That a chapter in the book is poetic does not make the whole book

01: WHY WE NEED TO INTERPRET SCRIPTURE

poetic, any more than the poetry in Genesis 49, Exodus 15, Numbers 23-24, or Deuteronomy 32 and 33 makes those books poetic The absence of specific historical references is not that unusual in prophetic books. The book of Malachi does not contain any specific reference to the time it was written.

More importantly, Jesus describes Jonah as a real person who performed real actions. To make Jonah a literary fiction discredits Jesus' perfection.

> Then some of the Pharisees and teachers of the law said to him, "Teacher, we want to see a sign from you."
>
> He answered, "A wicked and adulterous generation asks for a sign! But none will be given it except the sign of the prophet Jonah. For as Jonah *was* three days and three nights in the belly of a huge fish, so the Son of Man *will be* three days and three nights in the heart of the earth. The men of Nineveh *will stand up at the judgment* with this generation and condemn it; for *they repented* at the preaching of Jonah, and now something greater than Jonah is here. (Matthew 12:38-41, *emphasis added*)

The men of Nineveh could hardly condemn Jesus' generation if the events in Jonah had never actually happened. If the events did not occur, they were never convicted of sin nor did they repent through Jonah's preaching. Jesus would be unlikely to use a fictional character's days in a fish as a comparison to His own burial and resurrection. Jesus' own words are that Jonah *was* in the belly of a huge fish. If it did not happen, a more accurate statement would be, "As Jonah was portrayed as being in the belly of a huge fish..."

Literary analysis also helps us consider whether we are dealing with figures of speech. We see similes, metaphors, allegories, anthropomorphisms, hyperboles, parables, and apocalyptic language in Scripture. We would miss the meaning of a passage if we took a figure of speech as though it were a literal statement.

It is common for those who intend to discredit the accuracy of Scripture to use figures of speech as evidence that the text cannot be objectively true. But all good writing, even good history, uses non-literal imagery to tell the story. When the text says that Jesus went through all the towns and villages, are we supposed to understand that to mean that He visited every single village? That statement is clearly meant to be hyperbolic. There are numerous similar examples.

But we must also avoid the opposite error and be careful not to salvage our dearly held theological positions by calling what is literal a figure of speech. Unfortunately, we can misinterpret figures of speech in both directions, by reading the figurative as literal and the literal as figurative. We see this most often when interpreting passages related to the end of the world. There is no denying that the task is difficult, with so many passages being filled with imagery. But when imagery is used literally, to create an interpretation that could only be arrived at in our particular time, with our particular culture, and with our particular technology, we have gone astray.

Equally, when a passage that lacks imagery is interpreted as hyperbole, in the absence of exaggerated language, we have missed the point of the text. These failures usually occur when our pre-existing assumptions bump into texts that deny our interpretation. Sadly, it is easier to force the biblical text to support our view than to re-examine and correct the flaw in the position we hold.

PERSONIFICATION

Another form of non-literal language is personification (taking something non-human and assigning it human characteristics). This language is found throughout the Old Testament.

> You will go out in joy
> and be led forth in peace;
> the mountains and hills
> will burst into song before you,
> and all the trees of the field
> will clap their hands. (Isaiah 55:12)

01: WHY WE NEED TO INTERPRET SCRIPTURE

The point of the Isaiah passage is not to suggest that mountains sing or that trees have hands to clap. The imagery is a literary vehicle that intends to describe extreme joy.

We see this too in the examples of talking animals, such as Balaam's donkey or the serpent in the garden of Eden. Those who deny the possibility of miracles immediately write off those biblical accounts as fables or superstition. But when our assumptions attempt to limit how God interacts with the world, they can alienate us from God's Word. If we take the biblical text seriously, in the absence of any indicators that a passage is not literal or that it intends to present fiction, we do have to believe that in certain situations animals spoke.

METAPHOR

When metaphors are used in Scripture, a word or phrase literally denoting one kind of object or idea is used in place of another to suggest a likeness or analogy between them (as in "drowning in money").

A metaphor paints a picture that helps us understand a concept or role more clearly. , but these images give us a better understanding of who He is and what He came to do through the Incarnation

But like other figures of speech, a metaphor can be problematic if it is taken as though it was intended to be a literal equation rather than a likeness. Also, metaphors can sometimes be complex, so it can be difficult to discern the exact point being made.

When, at the Last Supper, Jesus said, "This is my body," he was using a metaphor, but we are left with a challenge: how should we understand that metaphor? Was Jesus saying "This is my body—I have miraculously turned the bread and wine into my body, here and now?" Was He saying "This is my body—symbolically representing my physical death?" Christians have held many different views that run across the spectrum from the actual body being present in communion, to a spiritual presence in the ceremony, to the celebration of communion being pure representation with no physical or spiritual presence. Metaphors can be difficult to interpret.

MULTIPLE APPLICATIONS

Have you ever reread a passage and gotten something different out of it than what you'd gotten out of it before? If we study a text and determine its meaning, the same text can affect us differently as we grow, change, mature, or just face different life circumstances.

Passages about handling money may not mean much when we are poor and barely scraping by. But a few years later, when our finances improve, we may be struck by verses that tell us to use worldly wealth to gain friends for ourselves, so that when it is gone, we will be welcomed into eternal dwellings.

There is nothing wrong with seeing new things in the text as we change. The actual meaning of the text does not change, but its significance to us can change as we gain new insights and recognize things we did not see before.

GRAMMATICO-HISTORICAL METHOD

Sometimes grammar and the forms of words used can be crucial to understanding the meaning of a passage. If we were aware of the underlying Greek language, it could affect how we interpret a text. For example, in John 21:15–19 Jesus asks Peter three times if Peter loves Him. In the English version we get the impression that Peter is upset solely because Jesus asked three times. But in the Greek text, Jesus asks Peter twice if he *agape*'s Him (love like the love of God), and Peter, properly humbled, says he *philo*'s Him (love of a dear friend). The third time Jesus asks Peter if he *philo*'s Him. But Peter has already affirmed twice that he *philo*'s Jesus, so he is upset that Jesus would ask what he has already answered, but he vigorously affirms it again.

We should observe that the English translations do a good job of giving us access to the biblical text. So while we may not read Greek or Hebrew, God's Word is still available to us.

If we want to dig deeper into the text, Ancient Greek language classes are available through churches, secular universities, and Christian seminaries and universities. Hebrew courses are more difficult, but not impossible to find. There are also resources such as Logos software that can give us access to material in the original languages.

01: WHY WE NEED TO INTERPRET SCRIPTURE

HISTORICAL ANALYSIS

Historical analysis considers the setting and situation of a particular book in its historical context. Knowing things like who wrote a book, under what circumstances, and when in history can add clarity as we try to understand the issues addressed in the book. This information can be found in commentaries, Bible Handbooks, or Bible Almanacs.

AUTHORSHIP AND DATING

Similarly, knowing who wrote specific books and when is important for a number of reasons. Some scholars date prophetic books after the events they prophesy so as to discredit the idea that a prophet foretold the future. A good example of that is the book of Daniel, which some date almost 200 years after the time of Alexander the Great (around 167 BC), which is around the time Rome came into ascendency. This, in spite of the internal evidence that Daniel claims to have been written in the sixth century BC. It is necessary for sceptics to assume a later date, or they would have to acknowledge that Daniel precisely prophesied the world empires that arose from Babylon, to Persia, to Greece and Rome.

Things like the date Revelation was written or who wrote First and Second Peter would impact how we interpret Scripture. If Revelation was written later, views like Preterism would be discredited. If Peter did not write Second Peter it would raise questions about who did write it and if it had apostolic authority.

The question is asked, if Peter wrote First and Second Peter, why is the grammar and language so different between the two books? Those differences are used to argue that the books were written by two different people.

But it is not very hard to explain why the style and vocabulary in the two books is different. Peter says in Chapter 5 of I Peter that he has written by Silvanus, indicating that he did not personally write I Peter. Silvanus was an amanuensis who took Peter's words and wrote them down using his excellent writing skills. In II Peter, the language is cruder and the book was probably written by Peter himself.

Tools like these can help us remove the filters that keep us from seeing Scripture clearly and interpreting it accurately. In the next chapter we'll deepen our study and explore some new techniques that will help us see God's Word more clearly still.

02

PRACTICAL RULES

We read the Bible using the same rules we use for any book. The words and language of the text provide meaning in the same way words and sentences are meaningful in any other book. The Bible is special because it is inspired and inerrant, but it is not a magic talisman used to get individual answers to specific situations.

What is ordinary about the Bible is that it is written in human languages, using the words and styles of the authors. The words are consistent with the vocabulary of the authors. The original text can be translated into other languages so that the meaning is understandable. The types of writings—historical narrative, poetry, and instruction—are similar to secular writings of history, poetry, and instruction.

But this text is the Word of God, and that is not ordinary. The content of the book becomes clearer as the Holy Spirit works in us to show us how we can apply a passage to our lives. As we take the objective meaning of the words in a text and learn how they impact our thoughts and actions, it is critical that we pray and depend upon the Spirit.

Because the Bible is such an extraordinary book, people tend to handle it in ways they would not think of using for other books. Someone might take a phrase as his verse for the day and make it answer the most pressing question in his life. Some people search for answers by "depending on the Spirit"—

sticking their fingers in a random verse and hoping for a divine response.

CAN THESE APPROACHES WORK?

It is possible that these approaches could work, but any success would be entirely due to the mercy of God. These approaches are magical thinking, and do not treat the Bible appropriately. It is just as likely that these approaches could have devastating consequences. The content in the Scriptures calls for careful study before we can recognize the principles discussed and determine what we should do in response.

READING THE BIBLE EXISTENTIALLY

I describe this as entering into the biblical account. To do this, we walk alongside the biblical figures as they go through trials, make decisions, and live life. In all this, we take the record of the biblical events seriously. People often read the Bible in a way that creates a fairyland world, where people do things that no real person would ever do. We accept what we have always heard, rather than questioning an unreasonable interpretation. I am not saying we should question the accuracy of the text, but that we should resist bringing unrealistic ideas and interpretations to our reading of Scripture.

Engaging with the Real Events in the Biblical Text

Two things happen when we read the Bible as though it was not describing real events. First, we miss the drama, tension, and excitement of God's work in the lives of people. People often complain that the Bible is boring, and it is no wonder when they gloss over the events in the text in a way that ignores a human drama to which we can relate. We almost yawn as we read about the terrifying experiences of people facing immanent death.

For example, consider the Israelites' escape from slavery in Egypt and their journey through the Red Sea. The Israelites were finally free from brutal slavery, and as they prepared to leave, the Egyptians gave them treasures to take with them. After traveling a number of days into the desert, the Israelites saw the Egyptians pursuing them. They observed how God put a cloud and a pillar of fire between them and the Egyptian troops. They walked through

02: PRACTICAL RULES

the Red Sea on dry land.

We know the events, but do we put ourselves into the biblical account? Can we imagine the joy not only of freedom, but of receiving goods from the Egyptians who had held them in slavery? How many days of walking or riding did it take for the huge number of Israelites to get to the Red Sea? Imagine the difficulty of ensuring that everyone had food and water. The elderly and physically disabled had to be cared for each day. Do we think about how terrified the people must have been when they first saw signs of pursuit? What did they think about the cloud and the pillar of fire that kept the Egyptians away? Were they afraid that the cloud would go away, leaving them exposed? As they took their first tentative steps into the Red Sea and saw the water piled up to make a path for them, how intense was their fear? Imagine how their dread of the Egyptians disappeared as the waters flooded over their enemies.

When we read the Bible, fully engaging with the biblical account, it comes to life for us. There is nothing boring about the joy of freedom, the terror of a pursuing enemy, the fear of walking through the middle of a large body of water, or the joy of seeing an opposing military force destroyed.

ACCEPTING MAGICAL IDEAS ABOUT REAL EVENTS

The second thing that happens when we read the Bible as though it does not describe real events is that we accept impossible things as true. I am not talking about miracles, but about our tendency to accept what I call "the Sunday school version of the Bible," which is filled with things inconsistent with the text.

It is interesting to see how people view David's battle with Goliath. Many people picture David as very young, perhaps a teenager, at the time he fought the giant. What happens when we put ourselves into the biblical account? The Sunday school version we already know trains us to gloss over unreasonable ideas.

So, while the reader would not allow their teenager to attack and kill a bear or a lion (which David did before he fought Goliath), they think David's parents were fine with their teen or preteen attacking bears and lions. Can you hear the discussion around the kitchen table? "Now David, when you are guarding the flocks, if a bear attacks the sheep, kill it! Or if a lion attacks the sheep, kill it!"

We could think that things were different back then. Perhaps it was normal for children and teens to attack bears and lions. It is magical thinking that imagines parents in biblical times were not as concerned for their children and were more willing to put their children in danger than we are. Let's think about what weapons the child would use. Arrows, spears and a sling could hurt a wild animal but an inexperienced warrior would not be likely to handle those weapons in a way that killed the animal with the first shot. A wounded animal would be much more dangerous. Additionally, people were smaller then than now, making it much harder to use a sword to kill a bear or lion.

In this magical world, the adults—who are afraid of the giant—send a young boy to fight this huge, seasoned warrior, who has with him an armor bearer. The fact that such a thing would never happen in the real world should send us back to the biblical account, which is so different from the Sunday school version.

Consider these verses:

> All the days of Saul there was bitter war with the Philistines, and whenever Saul saw a mighty or brave man, he took him into his service. (1 Samuel 14:52)

> One of the servants answered, "I have seen a son of Jesse of Bethlehem who knows how to play the lyre. He is a *brave man* and *a warrior*. He speaks well and is a fine-looking man. And the Lord is with him."
>
> Then Saul sent messengers to Jesse and said, "Send me your son David, who is with the sheep." So Jesse took a donkey loaded with bread, a skin of wine and a young goat and sent them with his son David to Saul.

02: PRACTICAL RULES

David came to Saul and entered his service. Saul liked him very much, and *David became one of his armor-bearers.* Then Saul sent word to Jesse, saying, "Allow David to remain in my service, for I am pleased with him." (1 Samuel 16:18–22, *emphasis added*)

Saul was afraid of David, because the Lord was with David but had departed from Saul. So he sent David away from him and *gave him command over a thousand men,* and David led the troops in their campaigns. (1 Samuel 18:12–13, *emphasis added*)

A careful reading of the passages surrounding the account of David and Goliath should change our view of this event. We see that David was, in fact, an accomplished warrior himself. David is described as a brave man and a warrior, and he became one of Saul's armor bearers before he fought Goliath. In 1 Samuel 18, we see that David was made a commander of one thousand men shortly after his battle with Goliath; later in the chapter, David marries Saul's daughter.

We need to read the biblical accounts as though they describe real people, living real lives, often in difficult circumstances. Instead of thinking we already know what happened in one of our familiar Bible stories, we need to read the biblical account. We can't just read a snippet that might reinforce our pre-existing view. We need to read about David, the brave warrior and armor bearer for King Saul, before he fought Goliath. That might give us pause as we think about David's age.

This close reading shows us that David was not a little boy throwing rocks at a giant, but rather a warrior, an underdog who relied on God to help him defeat a powerful foe. When we see David as an adult fighting Goliath it changes our application of the passage to our own lives.

We see from this passage that when we are underdogs, fighting against people, institutions, or circumstances that require us to depend upon God, we can look to David who overcame a giant obstacle with God's help.

HOW TO SEE: READING GOD'S WORD WITH NEW EYES

FACING OUR PREJUDICES

It is also important for us to understand what we bring to our reading of the biblical text. We may not like what we read and may need to deal with our prejudices. Asking, "Why does God do this?" or "Why does Scripture say this?" can help us process those passages where God appears to be unfair, harsh, or cruel. Our sinful nature makes it harder for us to even think that someone who disagrees with our opinions could be intelligent, insightful, or possibly even correct, but people who disagree with God's Word may simply bring bad presuppositions to the table. They can undervalue God's Word and still be discerning and observe things that are true.

We are often quicker to extend the benefit of the doubt to ourselves than we are to extend it others. When someone sins against us, we are outraged at their malice, but when we sin against others, we argue that we made a mistake. We do this in our relationships, but we can also do this when evaluating parts of the biblical text. If I reject the idea that some people go to hell, I may attribute evil attitudes and thoughts to someone who teaches on hell. I may not read parts of the text that speak about hell, or I may even impugn the character of the biblical writer.

We may not do this in a direct a manner. We may soften our approach and believe, or even say, that the one teaching the view we do not hold is merely confused or ignorant. But we cannot allow biases to justify our judgment and rejection of what is in the text.

HOW CAN WE IDENTIFY BIASES THAT AFFECT OUR UNDERSTANDING OF THE BIBLICAL TEXT?

There are a number of ways we can see our biases. Do we honestly look at the alternate position? Are we ready to read the biblical text in context in order to get the objective meaning of the text, no matter where it leads? If we do this with integrity, we are more likely to get to the truth.

In contrast, do we throw up objections that lack logical validity? I once had an apologist for a particular eschatological position say that some unknown scholar had determined that the imagery in Revelation could not draw its meaning from the same image appearing elsewhere in Scripture.

He made the statement as though that settled the matter. Since I had just published a book that showed how the imagery in Revelation was found in other parts of Scripture and drew its meaning from those other passages, I knew from my own thorough, recent study, that his statement was logically flawed. What he could have said, if he was being honest, was that a scholar had determined that comparison of the imagery in Revelation to the same images appearing elsewhere in Scripture resulted in a contradiction of the position he was trying to defend.

Do we look at our opponent's position simply to prove them wrong? If they happen to be right, we will never see it. It is difficult work, but we should make the effort to eliminate our biases.

INTERACTING WITH THE WORDS OF JESUS

While we are busy viewing the Bible as a good luck charm, or as we explain away the things we don't like or agree with, we often don't take seriously some of the statements of Jesus. For example, consider what Jesus says in Matthew 24:15-21:

> So when you see standing in the holy place "the abomination that causes desolation," spoken of through the prophet Daniel—let the reader understand—then let those who are in Judea flee to the mountains. Let no one on the housetop go down to take anything out of the house. Let no one in the field go back to get their cloak. How dreadful it will be in those days for pregnant women and nursing mothers! *Pray that your flight will not take place in winter or on the Sabbath.* For then there will be great distress, unequaled from the beginning of the world until now—and never to be equaled again. (*emphasis added*)

Jesus commands us to pray that the events He describes in Matthew 24 will not take place in winter or on a Sabbath. Have we prayed this prayer? If we truly took the words of Jesus seriously and believed that the Lord would come back soon, would it not be important to pray that prayer?

Or in a similar vein, consider Matthew 24:10–13:

At that time many will turn away from the faith and will betray and hate each other, and many false prophets will appear and deceive many people. *Because of the increase of wickedness, the love of most will grow cold,* but the one who stands firm to the end will be saved. (emphasis added)

Jesus tells us that at the end, the love of most will grow cold. We can shrug our shoulders and say, "Isn't that a shame." Or we can take it seriously. Recall Abraham, who, when told that Sodom was going to be destroyed, negotiated with God. He asked God, "Will you sweep away the righteous with the wicked?" (Gen. 18:23) From that point Abraham, starting with fifty righteous, progressively reduced the number of righteous people in Sodom until God agreed that for ten righteous people, He would not destroy the city.

Does it grieve you that at the end, the love of most (believers) will grow cold? If so, perhaps we all should begin negotiating with God.

As we learn to identify and remove the obstacles that prevent us from reading the Bible clearly, we'll likely find ourselves taking His words more seriously. But understanding what He says is different from understanding what He means. For that, we'll need a tool that helps us interpret God's Word.

03

THE CLAP METHOD

Much of what I have to say in this book can be found in other books on hermeneutics. Yet, sadly, many people read those other books and still miss the target in interpreting Scripture. I believe the reason for this is that we get in the way of understanding what is in the biblical text.

The following series of rules, designed to supplement the standard interpretive rules, are intended to help us address our self-imposed blindness to what is going on in the text. I have organized these rules under the acronym *CLAP*.

CONTEXT

The C in CLAP stands for *Context*. All good books about studying the Bible emphasize the importance of context—this concept is not new or different. We must always consider the context of the passage we study. No verse ever teaches something completely inconsistent with the surrounding verses. In many cases, what is difficult to understand in one verse is explained in a previous verse or chapter. Sometimes, the context can even be in another book of the Bible. Let's consider a number of examples.

In Ezekiel 37:9, a breath from God breathes into the "slain" and brings them to life. Nothing in Ezekiel 37 specifically indicates how the dry bones died. Yet Ezekiel describes them as slain. How does he know that they were slain? In chapter 33, Jerusalem has fallen, yet the people say, "Abraham was only one man, yet he possessed the land. But we are many; surely the land has been given to us as our possession" (v. 24). The Lord points out their sins (they do not walk by faith like Abraham), so those in the ruins will die by the sword, those in the country will be devoured by wild animals, and those in strongholds will die of the plague. They are slain by the Lord. Yet, when Israel loses all hope, God promises that He will raise them up and then they will know that He is the Lord. He raises the slain to new life in Ezekiel 37. Knowing the context of this passage helps us understand why Ezekiel calls the dry bones "slain."

Another example is found in 1 Corinthians.

> If I speak in the tongues of men or of angels, but do not have love, I am only a resounding gong or a clanging cymbal. If I have the gift of prophecy and can fathom all mysteries and all knowledge, and if I have a faith that can move mountains, but do not have love, I am nothing. If I give all I possess to the poor and give over my body to hardship that I may boast, but do not have love, I gain nothing.
>
> Love is patient, love is kind. It does not envy, it *does not boast*, it *is not proud*. It does not dishonor others, it *is not self-seeking*, it is not easily angered, it keeps no record of wrongs. Love does not delight in evil but rejoices with the truth. It always protects, always trusts, always hopes, always perseveres.
>
> Love never fails. But where there are prophecies, they will cease; where there are tongues, they will be stilled; *where there is knowledge, it will pass away*. For we know in part and we prophesy in part, but when completeness comes, what is in part disappears. When I was a child, I talked like a child, I thought like a child, I reasoned like a child. When I became a man, I put the ways of childhood behind me. For now we see only a reflection as in a mirror; then we shall see face to face. Now I know in part; then I shall know fully, even as I am fully known. And now these three remain: faith, hope and love. But the greatest of these is love. (1 Corinthians 13:1–13,* *emphasis added*)

03: THE CLAP METHOD

The context of this passage clarifies the meaning of these verses. While American Christians regularly use this chapter in weddings because it so wonderfully describes love, it is unlikely the Corinthians did the same. When the Corinthians read this letter from Paul, they probably read it in one sitting. When Paul got to the "love" chapter, the Corinthians were not happy about what they read. The very things Paul says love is are the things he has already told the Corinthians they are not.

> You are still *worldly*. For since there is jealousy and quarreling among you, are you not *worldly*? Are you not acting like mere humans? (1 Corinthians 3:3, *emphasis added*)

> Now, brothers, I have applied these things to myself and Apollos for your benefit, so that you may learn from us the meaning of the saying, "Do not go beyond what is written." Then you will not take *pride* in one man over against another. For who makes you different from anyone else? What do you have that you did not receive? And if you did receive it, why do you *boast* as though you did not? (1 Corinthians 4:6-7, *emphasis added*)

> Some of you have become *arrogant*, as if I were not coming to you. But I will come to you very soon, if the Lord is willing, and then I will find out not only how these *arrogant* people are talking, but what power they have. (1 Corinthians 4:18-17, *emphasis added*)

> And you are *proud*! Shouldn't you rather have been filled with grief and have put out of your fellowship the man who did this? Even though I am not physically present, I am with you in spirit. And I have already passed judgment on the one who did this, just as if I were present. When you are assembled in the name of our Lord Jesus and I am with you in spirit, and the power of our Lord Jesus is present, hand this man over to Satan, so that the sinful nature may be destroyed and his spirit saved on the day of the Lord. Your *boasting* is not good. Don't you

know that a little yeast works through the whole batch of dough? (1 Corinthians 5:2–6, *emphasis added*)

Now about food sacrificed to idols: We know that we all possess knowledge. *Knowledge puffs up*, but love builds up. The man who *thinks he knows something* does not yet know as he ought to know. But the man who loves God is known by God. (1 Corinthians 8:1–3, *emphasis added*)

When read in isolation, 1 Corinthians 13 seems to be a beautiful chapter about love, but the same passage read in context is an indictment of the Corinthians. And if it is an indictment of the Corinthians, is it not likely to also be an indictment of us? Where envy, jealousy, pride, arrogance, and glorying in knowledge live in the church, this chapter holds such behavior up to a mirror to show how different it is from the love that should live in our hearts and in our midst.

Context is especially important in image-filled books like Revelation. The context for many passages in Revelation lies in other books of the Bible, which makes this book a difficult one to interpret—to do it well, we need to really know the whole Bible. So, let's look at Revelation 20.

And when the thousand years are ended, Satan will be released from his prison and will come out to deceive the nations that are at the four corners of the earth, *Gog and Magog,* to gather them for battle; *their number is like the sand of the sea.* (Revelation 20:7–8 ESV, *emphasis added*)

IF WE LOOK AT THE PHRASE "GOG AND MAGOG," HOW DOES IT FIT INTO THE FLOW OF THE PASSAGE?

Clearly, it is a completely out-of-context insertion into the text. Gog and Magog are not nations at the four corners of the earth. The point of the insertion is to point to another passage in Scripture.

> Therefore, son of man, prophesy, and say to Gog, Thus says the Lord God: On that day when my people Israel are dwelling securely, will you not know it? You will come from your place out of the uttermost parts of the north, you and many peoples with you, all of them riding on horses, *a great host, a mighty army.* You will come up against my people Israel, *like a cloud covering the land. In the latter days* I will bring you against my land, that the nations may know me, when through you, O Gog, I vindicate my holiness before their eyes. (Ezekiel 38:14–16 ESV, *emphasis added*)

John makes the connection for us with that simple insertion, and we know that what he is describing in Revelation 20 is the same thing prophesied in Ezekiel 38. The simile comparing the numbers of people to the sand of the sea in Revelation is paralleled using different simile (cloud covering the land) in Ezekiel.

In the same way, we can find the context for portions of Judges 2 in the book of Joshua. The challenge is to know your Bible well enough that as you read the Judges passage, you will be reminded of you what you may have just read in Joshua 24.

> But Joshua said to the people, "You are not able to serve the Lord, for he is a holy God. He is a jealous God; he will not forgive your transgressions or your sins. If you forsake the Lord and serve foreign gods, then he will turn and do you harm and consume you, after having done you good." And the people said to Joshua, "No, but we will serve the Lord." Then Joshua said to the people, "You are witnesses against yourselves that you have chosen the Lord, to serve him." And they said, "We are witnesses." He said, "Then put away the foreign gods that are among you, and incline your heart to the Lord, the God of Israel." And the people said to Joshua, "The Lord our God we will serve, and his voice we will obey." So Joshua made a covenant with the people that day, and put in place statutes and rules for them at Shechem. (Joshua 24:19–25 ESV)

Before Joshua's death, he warns Israel, and they covenant to follow the Lord. After such an inspiring event, where the people promise to serve the Lord, we might hope that the people would remain faithful for a long time. However, that was not to be.

> When Joshua dismissed the people, the people of Israel went each to his inheritance to take possession of the land. And the people served the Lord all the days of Joshua, and all the days of the elders who outlived Joshua, who had seen all the great work that the Lord had done for Israel. And Joshua the son of Nun, the servant of the Lord, died at the age of 110 years. And they buried him within the boundaries of his inheritance in Timnath-heres, in the hill country of Ephraim, north of the mountain of Gaash. And all that generation also were gathered to their fathers. *And there arose another generation after them who did not know the Lord or the work that he had done for Israel.* (Judges 2:6–10 ESV, *emphasis added*)

It is fine to say "we will follow the Lord," but part of that means teaching our children so they know the Lord as well. The context of Judges 2:6–10 is Joshua 24:19–25, because the significance of a generation arising which does not know the Lord is that the previous generation, which had promised to faithfully serve the Lord, failed to instruct the next generation.

LOOK FOR WHAT IS SURPRISING

The second letter in CLAP is L, which tells us to *Look for what is surprising*.

When we read the Bible, we often see only what we always saw. We know the stories. As mentioned earlier, many of us have learned the Sunday school version of the Bible. But be warned: the Sunday school version of the Bible is often an out-of-context presentation of portions of stories.

We know Daniel and the lion's den. But do we know what happened to the men who accused Daniel along with their families? We need to look for things that are hard to explain. Too often we read what we already think we know the passage says, rather than what is in the text. Passages that we have heard and read many times, and that we may even have studied or taught, may contain important points we have missed. Often, what we're sure the text says is not what it actually says. We need to look for things in the text that are surprising.

Are you surprised when you read that after Jesus had not eaten for forty days, he became hungry (Matthew 4:2)? To understand why, we may need to look outside the Scriptures, at some resources related to human biology, to understand how that can be.

Is it surprising that Jesus stated that He needed to be baptized by John in order to fulfill all righteousness? The Scriptures teach us that John's baptism was different than Christian baptism (Acts 19:3-7). The same passage tells us that John's baptism was a baptism of repentance, which Jesus clearly did not need. So why did Jesus need to be baptized by John?

Is it surprising that Jesus chose Judas? Jesus knew from the beginning who was going to betray Him (John 6:64-71). Why would Jesus choose a disciple He knew would betray Him? If Jesus intentionally chose His betrayer, what does that say about free will and predestination?

These are but a few of the hundreds of surprising things we see in Scripture. What is surprising to me may not be surprising to you—and vice versa. Just the other day, I was surprised that King David attributed his devotion to God to his mother. We all know David's father, Jesse, but David's mother is not named in Scripture. Yet David says,

> Turn to me and have mercy on me;
> show your strength in behalf of your servant;
> save me, because I serve you
> just as my mother did. (Psalm 86:16)

> Truly I am your servant, Lord;
> I serve you just as my mother did;
> you have freed me from my chains. (Psalm 116:16)

If we want to recognize in Scripture those things which are surprising, we must be alert as we read, and we must desire to get the most out of Scripture. When we find things that surprise us, those discoveries energize our study of Scripture, which then can inspire us to greater love and devotion toward God.

ASK DIFFICULT QUESTIONS

The letter A in CLAP stands for *Ask difficult questions.* If we read the Bible as though we already know what it says, we may not see any difficult questions. But just as a careful reading of the text will show us things that are surprising, it will also present us with difficult questions. If we have eyes to see and ears to hear, there will be difficult questions to answer.

BUT ARE WE WILLING TO ASK TOUGH QUESTIONS OF THE TEXT?

I don't know exactly why we are hesitant to ask tough questions of the text. Is it because we are afraid that we don't know enough or that we could be led astray? Are we intimidated by the idea that wise men have already decided what the text means? Do we think asking the text and God tough questions is sinful or disrespectful?

Whatever the reason, most people hesitate to explore some of the unexpected things they see in the text. By unexpected, I am not thinking merely of the surprising things we see. There are many things in Scripture that we know about and don't find surprising, yet we don't really understand God's purpose and are not willing to ask.

These questions surface as we read the text and find God doing things that seem unlike the God we know. The benefit of asking these questions is that we may get to know God better. We often emphasize one element of God's character so much that we undervalue or avoid entirely another element. But God's perfections are like an infinitely-sided diamond: one facet may sparkle, but we miss out if we don't look at all the sides.

03: THE CLAP METHOD

GOD, WHY DID YOU TELL ISRAEL TO KILL ALL THE PEOPLE, INCLUDING CHILDREN, IN SOME OF THE CITIES THEY CAPTURED?

As for Makkedah, Joshua captured it on that day and struck it, and its king, with the edge of the sword. He devoted to destruction every person in it; he left none remaining. And he did to the king of Makkedah just as he had done to the king of Jericho. Then Joshua and all Israel with him passed on from Makkedah to Libnah and fought against Libnah. And the Lord gave it also and its king into the hand of Israel. And he struck it with the edge of the sword, and every person in it; he left none remaining in it. And he did to its king as he had done to the king of Jericho. Then Joshua and all Israel with him passed on from Libnah to Lachish and laid siege to it and fought against it. And the Lord gave Lachish into the hand of Israel, and he captured it on the second day and struck it with the edge of the sword, and every person in it, as he had done to Libnah. (Joshua 10:28–32 ESV)

To kill every single person seems harsh. Yet God is perfect in all He does. We need to ask the question above so we can begin to grasp the truth that God is more than just a feel-good, loving God. This apparent harshness might give us insight into other attributes of God, such as His justice, holiness, and wrath. It might also correct the ideas we have that are untrue. It would be hard to read the passage above and state that God loves unconditionally.

Some of the difficult questions we ask may be answered, to a greater or lesser extent, in theology textbooks. Of course, two different books may offer two different answers, and sorting out the correct answer may require a good deal of work. The payoff again is that we get to know God better.

We may want to avoid controversy. There are so many complex theological questions it can seem impossible for us to resolve issues on which brilliant theologians disagree.

The thing is, asking difficult questions does not always lead us to complete and satisfying answers. Sometimes the challenge is merely to stop ignoring parts of God's Word. Do we gloss over passages that appear to teach something different than what we believe? Regardless of what we believe, we dishonor God and His communication with us if we minimize passages that might raise questions about our existing beliefs. Whatever we believe about predestination and free will, we cannot deny that the biblical text says God predestined us for adoption. Can we ask a difficult question and try to understand what Scripture is teaching us?

GOD, IF SOME ARE PREDESTINED AND CHOSEN BEFORE THE FOUNDATION OF THE EARTH WHY DO YOU HOLD ACCOUNTABLE THOSE WHO DO NOT FOLLOW YOU?

Blessed be the God and Father of our Lord Jesus Christ, who has blessed us in Christ with every spiritual blessing in the heavenly places, even as *he chose us in him before the foundation of the world*, that we should be holy and blameless before him. *In love he predestined us* for adoption to himself as sons through Jesus Christ, according to the purpose of his will, to the praise of his glorious grace, with which he has blessed us in the Beloved....

In him we have obtained an inheritance, *having been predestined* according to the purpose of him who works all things according to the counsel of his will, so that we who were the first to hope in Christ might be to the praise of his glory. (Ephesians 1:3–6, 11–12 ESV, *emphasis added*)

This is a difficult question, and we may never know the answer perfectly. The thing is, we can't ask questions like this and then do nothing else. If we ask tough questions, we can take one of two approaches. Some people are motivated to do intensive Bible study to try to find the answers. Other people will keep the question in the back of their minds as they read and study the Bible, and they will consider how certain passages answer the question.

03: THE CLAP METHOD

What is not helpful is when we take a question, put it in the back of our mind, and then harbor resentment toward God about the issue. In order to resent God, our minds must already be made up about the answer to the question. But if we have not yet answered the question, we don't know what we will discover about God. It is human nature to bring our sinful attitudes and thoughts to bear when we think we will not like what God is doing. How sad it is that we are willing to give sinful humans the benefit of the doubt, yet we judge God harshly. If we presume that the God who allowed Himself to be tortured to death for us is always working for our good, we will not permit bad circumstances to determine our attitude toward God.

We can supplement what we find in the Scriptures with other resources that present us with additional information. Our objective is to know the God of the Scriptures better.

PAY ATTENTION TO DETAILS

The letter P in CLAP stands for *Pay attention to details*. One would think that for something as important as the inspired Word of God, we would pay careful attention to what we read. Sadly, most believers miss the significant details in the passages with which we are most familiar—the Sunday school version of the Bible overrides what is actually in the text. Too often, we read the Bible with the idea that we already know what the words will say.

Reading the text carefully involves doing some things and avoiding others. Among the problems we face are:

- The tendency to think we have read the text and seen all it has to offer.
- The temptation to accept other peoples' descriptions of what the text says in place of reading the text, in its context, for ourselves.

We must read the text carefully, elevating our sensitivity to words, phrases, and verses that don't seem to fit what we have been reading. Our expectations and assumptions make things that should leap out at us quietly fade into the background.

MATTHEW 2

Let's consider some passages that illustrate the CLAP principles. In Matthew 2, wise men come to find the king of the Jews. We know the biblical account, since we have heard it read and preached at least once a year at Christmas. We know all about the wise men who followed the star, and *much of what we think we know is untrue.* The following two statements are *not* true.

- The wise men followed the star from their home to Bethlehem.
- The star was some sort of natural phenomenon.

Let's bring to bear what we have learned about CLAP. As you read the biblical account, see if anything in the passage surprises you. Do any difficult questions occur to you? What details might you have overlooked in the past?

After Jesus was born in Bethlehem in Judea, during the time of King Herod, Magi from the east came to Jerusalem and asked, "Where is the one who has been born king of the Jews? We saw his star when it rose and have come to worship him."

When King Herod heard this he was disturbed, and all Jerusalem with him. When he had called together all the people's chief priests and teachers of the law, he asked them where the Messiah was to be born. "In Bethlehem in Judea," they replied, "for this is what the prophet has written:

"'But you, Bethlehem, in the land of Judah, are by no means least among the rulers of Judah; for out of you will come a ruler who will shepherd my people Israel.'"

Then Herod called the Magi secretly and found out from them the exact time the star had appeared. He sent them to Bethlehem and said, "Go and search carefully for the child. As soon as you find him, report to me, so that I too may go and worship him."

After they had heard the king, they went on their way, and the star they had seen when it rose went ahead of them until it stopped over the place where the child was. When they saw the star, they were overjoyed. On coming to the house, they saw the child with his mother Mary, and they bowed down and worshiped him. Then they opened their treasures and presented him with gifts of gold, frankincense and myrrh. And having been warned in a dream not to go back to Herod, they returned to their country by another route. (Matthew 2:1-12)

Let's look at this passage closely, using the concepts in CLAP.

- *Look for what is surprising*: The wise men went to Jerusalem (v. 1). This is surprising because we tend to think that the wise men followed the star to Bethlehem.
- *Pay attention to details*: The wise men said they saw His star and had come to worship (v. 2). They did not say they had followed the star. We can see that they did not follow the star, because they came to Jerusalem and Jesus was not there.
- *Pay attention*: The wise men were told the child was to be born in Bethlehem (vv. 7-8). If we are paying attention to details, we might want to look up how far Bethlehem is from Jerusalem. It turns out that it is about five miles away.
- *Pay attention*: The star went ahead of the wise men when they left Jerusalem, and it led the wise men the five miles to Bethlehem (v. 9). This is surprising because it appears to disqualify any natural phenomenon. What comet or conjunction of planets could lead anyone over a journey of five miles?
- *Look*: When the wise men left Jerusalem and saw the star they were overjoyed (v. 10). If they had followed the star from Persia, seeing the star would be no big thing. If they had followed the star, they could have been irritated that it took them to the wrong place. Yet they are overjoyed when they see the star, which is an extreme response.
- *Ask difficult questions*: Were the wise men overjoyed when they saw the star and followed it as they left Jerusalem, or were they overjoyed that it stopped over the place where the child was? (v. 10)
- *Look*: It appears that the star the wise men followed to Bethlehem

was the same star they had first seen when they left Persia (v. 9). This same star somehow led them the final five miles to Bethlehem.
- *Pay attention*: If we pay attention to details, we observe that the wise men did not need a star to lead them to Bethlehem. It was, after all, only five miles away and the wise men had been told where they needed to go. So, when the text says the star stopped over the place where the child was (v. 9), and the wise men were overjoyed, it appears that the star actually led them to the house where Jesus lived. That would be a miraculous star.
- *Pay attention*: The wise men came to the house (v. 11), not to the manger. Unlike the manger scenes that are everywhere during the Christmas season, the wise men and the shepherds did not arrive to see Jesus on the same day. It is no surprise that Mary and Joseph had moved out of the stable and now lived in a house.
- *Context*: If we go beyond our passage to Matthew 2:16, we see additional details that reinforce the idea that the wise men did not arrive until more than a year after Jesus was born.
    When Herod realized that he had been outwitted by the Magi, he was furious, and he gave orders to kill all the boys in Bethlehem and its vicinity who were two years old and under, in accordance with the time he had learned from the Magi. (Matthew 2:16)
- *Pay attention*: Herod did not order newborns to be killed but children two or under (v. 16), indicating that Jesus may have been more than a year old when the wise men came.

I wonder how many of these bullet points told you something you already knew. You could find many of these in study guides and commentaries; some require you to read the text carefully. But if there was even one point here that you didn't know, that is significant. How often have we read this passage or heard it read? And if we can miss things from a passage we engage with at least once a year, what else are we missing in other biblical passages?

03: THE CLAP METHOD

SAMSON'S STRENGTH

Let's consider another example. Many of us are familiar with the biblical account of Samson and his great strength. Suppose we read the account of Samson and Delilah. What detail should we notice?

> Some time later, [Samson] fell in love with a woman in the Valley of Sorek whose name was Delilah. The rulers of the Philistines went to her and said, "See if you can lure him into showing you the secret of his great strength and how we can overpower him so we may tie him up and subdue him. Each one of us will give you eleven hundred shekels of silver."
> So Delilah said to Samson, "Tell me the secret of your great strength and how you can be tied up and subdued." (Judges 16:4–6)

Does this text match the picture you had in your mind about what Samson looked like? We tend to assign great strength to Samson based his physical attributes. We think of a huge man tearing a lion apart. But there would be no secret of Samson's great strength if he was well over six feet tall and weighed 250 pounds. Clearly, Samson was not a large, powerful man. He had a secret that gave him great strength. The secret was that the Spirit of God would come on him powerfully and he would do amazing feats of strength.

What is interesting in this passage is that the Philistines so firmly believed that Samson had a secret that they had Delilah ask Samson several times about the secret of his strength. Samson tells her things that are not true about the source of his strength yet she does not give up. The Philistines are not afraid of Samson's natural strength because they say that they can overpower him, tie him up, and subdue him if they find out the secret of his great strength. None of them look at Samson and conclude that his great strength comes from his physical attributes.

One important lesson of Samson (among others) is that God is able to equip us to do amazing things, beyond our native abilities. We miss this lesson if we think God used a strong man to impose his human power on God's enemies. We must read this passage without thinking that we already know what it says.

END TIMES

One of the areas where we most interpret the biblical text through our assumptions is in passages that teach about end times. Sadly, most eschatological interpretations depend on people who have read the text through the eyes of what they have been taught.

Many Christians are quick to ask other believers which position they hold about the second coming of the Lord. Are they pre-mil, a-mil, post-mil, or preterist? But once we ask which of the major positions someone holds, we have placed them in a box with all the trappings of that view. The problem with this is that every major eschatological position has some things wrong with its view.

Let's consider some examples of how we trap ourselves in an untenable position. A majority of Christians who believe in the Bible have been taught the Lord will return in an invisible, silent rapture. If that is supported by Scripture, we should whole heartedly embrace it. But what is the biblical language used of the return of Christ?

> "So if anyone tells you, 'There he is, out in the wilderness,' do not go out; or, 'Here he is, in the inner rooms,' do not believe it. For as *lightning that comes from the east is visible* even in the west, so will be the coming of the Son of Man.... And he will send his angels with a *loud trumpet call*, and they will gather his elect from the four winds, from one end of the heavens to the other." (Matthew 24:26–27, 31, *emphasis added*)

> Then he said to his disciples, "The time is coming when you will long to see one of the days of the Son of Man, but you will not see it. People will tell you, 'There he is!' or 'Here he is!' Do not go running off after them. For the Son of Man in his day will be like the *lightning, which flashes and lights up the sky from one end to the other*. But first he must suffer many things and be rejected by this generation. (Luke 17:22–25, *emphasis added*)

Listen, I tell you a mystery: We will not all sleep, but we will all be changed—in a flash, in the twinkling of an eye, at the last trumpet. For *the trumpet will sound*, the dead will be raised imperishable, and we will be changed. For the perishable must clothe itself with the imperishable, and the mortal with immortality. (1 Corinthians 15:51–53, *emphasis added*)

According to the Lord's word, we tell you that we who are still alive, who are left until the coming of the Lord, will certainly not precede those who have fallen asleep. For the Lord himself will come down from heaven, with *a loud command*, with *the voice of the archangel* and with *the trumpet call of God*, and the dead in Christ will rise first. After that, we who are still alive and are left will be caught up together with them in the clouds to meet the Lord in the air. And so we will be with the Lord forever. Therefore encourage one another with these words. (1 Thessalonians 4:15–18, *emphasis added*)

Here, outside of Revelation, are three references to Christ's return—in Matthew, 1 Corinthians, and 1 Thessalonians—that all say that it will be accompanied by a loud trumpet. Matthew and Luke both describe the return as visible, like lightning that flashes across the sky. Sometimes the loud and visible texts about Christ's return are dismissed as relating to a later return of Christ, after the silent rapture.

But if we pay attention to details, we will see that in the 1 Thessalonians passage Paul says "we who are still alive," potentially including himself with those awaiting this noisy return of Jesus. Additionally, Paul uses two other phrases that discredit an invisible, silent rapture. When Paul says "And so we will be with the Lord forever," he includes himself as potentially experiencing the noisy rapture. Again, at the end of the passage, he says, "Therefore encourage one another with these words." There would be no reason to encourage one another with these words about a loud and visible rapture if the only rapture these Thessalonians would experience was going to be silent and invisible. But so many people do not see this because they have been taught something different and have not paid attention to these details.

The principles in CLAP equip us to read Scripture well, sifting through the things we think we know to arrive at the truth of what Scripture says. Knowing the Context of the passage, Looking for things that surprise us, Asking good questions, and Paying attention to details—these skills will help us be thorough, thoughtful readers of God's Word.

04

PATTERNS IN SCRIPTURE

When studying a passage, it is helpful to look for patterns. Patterns are important because they highlight, through repetition, things that remain the same and things that change. Sometimes a word or a phrase and synonyms are repeated throughout a text. This repetition draws our attention to the writer's major points. At other times, what the writer leaves out may be the most revealing part of the text.

REPETITIONS

As an example, let's look for patterns in Revelation 2:1–3:22. This passage contains many repeated phrases, and the author makes many important points, through both what is repeated in the text and what is left out. Because we'll be studying a larger portion of Scripture here, you may want to print this passage out and highlight the phrases that are repeated in each letter to each church. A good exercise for a family to do together is to allow each member of the family to find a different repetition. Even young children can participate. Keep in mind that you are looking not only for the same words but also for themes that are repeated, even if different words are used.

In Revelation 2:1–3:22, there are many phrases and even whole sentences that are repeated for the seven churches. Compare what you found to what I found in this text:

1. To the angel of the church in …
2. These are the words of him who …
3. I know your deeds …
4. Yet I hold this against you …
5. He who has an ear, let him hear what the Spirit says to the churches …
6. To him who overcomes …

This passage demonstrates the importance of studying Revelation in its context by reading Revelation 1 before you get to Revelation 2. The phrase "These are the words of him who …" is normally followed by some reference to Jesus from Revelation 1. You would only recognize this connection if you had read chapter 1 first.

Additionally, if you continue to study Revelation, you will find that most of the things promised to "him who overcomes" in each church are found in Revelation 21 or 22.

I have intentionally overlooked one other pattern of repetition in Revelation 2 and 3 because it is more subtle and should be discussed separately. In addressing five of the churches, God acknowledges the suffering of the church. Ephesus is commended for hard work and perseverance. Smyrna is commended for facing afflictions, poverty, and slander, and the people there are warned that they are about to face prison and persecution. Pergamum is told that they have not renounced their faith even when one of their number was put to death. Thyatira has done service and shown perseverance. Philadelphia is weak, but has kept God's Word and not denied His name. They are to endure patiently.

There are two churches where suffering is not mentioned. To Sardis, God says, "I know your deeds; you have a reputation for being alive, but you are dead" (Rev. 3:1). To Laodicea, God says, "I am about to spit you out of my mouth" (Rev. 3:16). This pattern shows us the necessity of suffering. The church, when it is faithful, will suffer; when she is not suffering, she is not worthy of her God.

The repeated patterns in the letters to the churches emphasize those things that the universal church shares. We have common needs and common goals. We see patterns of promise, which are the hope and confidence of the church. These patterns emphasize the majesty and glory of God and show that we share the gifts of God (the Spirit and the Word of God) in common.

CONTEXT (LOOKING BACK)

This next passage was selected to allow you to work in a section where the main body of the text is dependent on what has gone before. Suppose we were going to study 2 Corinthians 4. We typically would begin in the first verse of the chapter and continue to the end. But reading 2 Corinthians 4 out of context like this could be confusing, since many of the verses in chapter 4 rely on the context of chapter 3.

In this exercise, you may want to once again print out our text, which is 2 Corinthians 3:1–4:18. You can underline words and synonyms that are repeated in chapter 3, and then see which of those words are also used in chapter 4. Once again, this exercise is suitable for children. Even if you have to read the passage to them, they can help you find the words that are repeated. Discuss why it is necessary to read chapter 3 before you go on to chapter 4.

In 2 Corinthians 3, you may have underlined the following words:

- ministry (six times)
- glory, glorious, radiance (these three words appear thirteen times all together)
- veil, unveiled (these two words appear five times)
- Spirit (six times)

You may have found other words as well, but these make a good start. In 2 Corinthians 4, you may have found no further references to the Spirit, while the themes of ministry, glory, and veiling all continue. Knowing what Paul said in chapter 3 helps us in our study of chapter 4.

When 2 Corinthians 4 begins, "Therefore, since...we have this ministry," we know exactly what ministry Paul is talking about, because he defined it in chapter 3. The references to the gospel being veiled in 4:3 continue the discussion of 2 Corinthians 3:13–18. And because we noted the many references to glory in chapter 3, we can better understand the discussion of the glory of Christ, of God, and our own glory in chapter 4. We are likely to misunderstand chapter 4 if we read it in isolation from chapter 3.

THEMES THAT FLOW THROUGH AN ACCOUNT

Suppose you were going to study the account of Jesus calming the wind and waves in Matthew 8:23–27.

> Then he got into the boat and his disciples followed him. Suddenly a furious storm came up on the lake, so that the waves swept over the boat. But Jesus was sleeping. The disciples went and woke him, saying, "Lord, save us! We're going to drown!"
>
> He replied, "You of little faith, why are you so afraid?"
>
> Then he got up and rebuked the winds and the waves, and it was completely calm. The men were amazed and asked, "What kind of man is this? Even the winds and the waves obey him!"

WHAT IS SURPRISING ABOUT VERSE 26?

Jesus says the disciples are of little faith and asks why they are afraid. This is surprising because it must have been a ferocious storm to have scared the disciples, at least a third of whom were experienced fishermen. Isn't it unreasonable for Jesus to chastise the disciples this way, since the storm was so powerful and dangerous?

But if you read Matthew 7:28–9:8 for context, consider what primary theme runs through each event. The only hint you should need is that the end of Matthew 7 summarizes the theme that will be carried through chapter 8 and into chapter 9. Once again you may want to print out the text and underline the places where this theme appears in all the passages that follow. You are looking not only for the specific word, but for other words that mean the same thing. Consider what the theme is and suggest words that fit with this theme.

As you likely found, the primary theme that runs through this text is authority. Jesus not only teaches with authority, but He demonstrates authority in many other ways. To the leper, Jesus says, "Be clean," because He has the authority to heal a leper. The centurion acknowledges Jesus' authority and His ability to heal, even from a distance, and Jesus commends him for his great faith. Jesus heals Peter's mother-in-law and many others, demonstrating that He has the authority even to cast out demons. Jesus has the authority to tell the disciple who wanted to bury his father, "Follow me." Then, in the account we are examining, Jesus shows that He has the authority to calm the storm. The next passage again shows His authority, because the demons "begged" him. He told the demons where they were allowed to go, and the townspeople came and "pleaded" with Him to leave, because they feared Him but also because they were dismayed at what He had done to their investment in pigs. In Matthew 9, Jesus exhibits the authority to forgive sins, and to heal a paralytic. When the crowd saw this, they were filled with awe and they praised God, "who had given such authority to men" (v. 8).

The reason Jesus is so frustrated with the disciples during the storm is that He has already shown them that He has divine authority. The disciples turn to Jesus to help them—"Lord, save us!" (Matt. 8:25)—but as they do so, they say "We're going to drown." They are not expressing faith in the Lord who has such authority that He is able to keep them safe. Their lack of faith and fear show that they still did not know who Jesus was, because if they did, they would have been fearless.

CONTRASTS

A study of 1 John 1–2 allows us to build on what we have already learned. Within 1 John 1:1–2:14, we see many related words and synonyms, but the text also uses antonyms and contrasting statements. Identifying these contrasts, in addition to the similarities, can be helpful. Once again, you can print the text and work through this passage to identify patterns. Underline repeated themes and contrasting themes. I have found at least eight different patterns, so this text offers many options.

As we said there are at least eight patterns that can be seen in this text. I will list the ones I found.

SIMILARITIES

- Words that emphasize the physical connection with Christ—heard, seen, looked at, appeared, touched.
- Words that speak of bearing witness—proclaim, testify, declare, confess.
- Fellowship with each other and with the Father and His Son.
- The repeated theme of sin.
- The theme of knowing God.

CONTRASTS

- The contrast between darkness and light.
- The contrast between the one who claims, says, or hates, versus the one who walks, confesses, obeys, and loves.
- The contrast between truth and lying or deceiving.

If we look at the big picture in this passage, we see a simple contrast. Our message is that Jesus was really present on earth, truly man and truly God. It is on this basis that we fellowship with other believers. Many people claim that they can continue in sin, by not obeying the Lord or by arguing that they have not sinned. They might claim to know and belong to God, but they may, at the same time, hate their brother. But the true believer walks in the light and in the truth. He confesses his sins, obeys the Lord, and loves his brother. He knows God and desires nothing more than to be in harmony and fellowship with God and with the people of God.

This is all present in the text, and it becomes visible to us when we take the time to look for patterns. Learning to recognize patterns like these can help us to see clearly what is in the text and can enrich our study of Scripture.

05

OTHER HELPFUL RULES

When we encounter a particularly difficult passage, it can be helpful to have a variety of study tools to draw from. In this chapter, we'll explore a few other tools that can help us see Scripture clearly.

INTERPRET HISTORICAL NARRATIVES USING BIBLICAL TEACHING MATERIAL

When we read historical narratives—books like the Gospels and Acts, that describe the flow of historical events—we notice that many of them contain teaching and instructional content. For example, the Gospels record Jesus' activities, but they also include many of his teachings. Most of these teachings need little, if any, interpretation from other parts of Scripture. But if some part of His teaching seems unclear to us, we can look up other helpful passages in the Bible and use a Scripture interprets Scripture approach to help us understand His teaching more clearly.

The point with this method is not to set Jesus' teaching against Paul's, or to prioritize one teaching over the other. We could only view it that way if the content of Scripture contained internal disagreements. But since we know that the text is inspired by God and we know that it has no conflicting voices, we can use Scripture's teaching passages to help us understand the historical events in Scripture.

For example, we can look at Jesus' activities and the events in the book of Acts and interpret how we should emulate them based on teaching from the Epistles. We are not Jesus and we are not called to the same ministry He had. We do not observe the Old Testament ceremonial law as Jesus did. At the same time, we need to determine what Jesus did that is required of us, versus the things Jesus did that we do not do—such as Jesus gathered twelve disciples into whom He poured His life.

> **ARE WE SUPPOSED TO DO THAT? HAVE WE HEARD PEOPLE TALK ABOUT FORMING GROUPS OF DISCIPLES? ARE WE SUPPOSED TO BECOME DISCIPLES OF SOMEONE ELSE?**

Paul's writings show us that he (Paul) did not gather twelve disciples. He did travel with others, and while he was the leader and primary speaker, in many ways he was a peer to those with him. In Acts 14:12, Paul is called Hermes (Mercury) because he is the speaker, but Barnabas is called Zeus, who was the king of the gods. Outsiders did not see Paul as dominating over the others in his party.

In the book of Acts, there are many events recorded that may or may not be things we should do. The Bible describes what happened, but does that description mean that the practice described is something we are also supposed to do? We should be careful not to take events recorded in the text and automatically make them a standard practice for the church today. If what is done in Acts is commended, and if Luke appears to be establishing a precedent for the church to follow, then it is more likely to be normative. We would hope that other biblical passages would provide support for that practice. But when a one-time event is described in Acts (such as taking handkerchiefs and aprons that touched an apostle to heal the sick and demon possessed – Acts 19:11f), that does not make whatever happened typical of what the church should do. This practice was never repeated in the biblical text and the practice is not commended by Scripture at all. Scripture describes what happened, but does not, in that description, suggest that it did or should ever happen again.

This principle does not apply only to New Testament passages but also to Old Testament texts. We must be careful not to hold up Old Testament saints as examples we are to follow, when the lesson in the text often teaches us to avoid the bad behavior of that saint. Additionally, we often copy things that occur in the Old Testament as though they are good, but those events are not always interpreted in the narrative—such as putting out a fleece, as Gideon did in the book of Judges. That is an interesting example, because Jesus responds to Satan by quoting Scripture that says, "Do not put God to the test" (Matthew 4:7). And there are many other passages in Scripture that speak of God's control of the world and the importance of trusting Him. In that case, we can see how biblical teaching material, drawn from other places in the Bible, can help us interpret the historical narrative of Gideon and the fleece.

THE IMPLICIT IS TO BE INTERPRETED BY THE EXPLICIT

By "implicit," I am referring to what appears to be implied by the text. In contrast, the explicit is what is literally said. We do not want to interpret biblical texts based on something we think the text might be saying. For this reason, the implicit is to be judged by the explicit. Another way to word this is to say we must judge the obscure by the clear. In some ways, this is a variation on the basic interpretive rule that we must not make assumptions.

We can use CLAP to help us handle the implicit and the explicit properly. If we don't pay attention to details, we could view something implicit as being explicit. If we are looking for what is surprising, we might hear the alarm bells go off when something unexpected happens, warning us that we missed something.

So, let's look at a passage where we might make assumptions. In a couple of passages, we see what appears to be God saying He will do something but then changing His mind or not doing what He said He was going to do. In the book of Jonah, God told Jonah to proclaim a particular message.

Jonah began by going a day's journey into the city, proclaiming, "Forty more days and Nineveh will be overthrown." (Jonah 3:4)

God's message was that He was going to destroy Nineveh. Yet God did not destroy the city.

When God saw what they did and how they turned from their evil ways, he relented and did not bring on them the destruction he had threatened. (Jonah 3:10)

It appears that God changed His mind. That might be the implication we draw from this passage. However, Scripture is clear that God does not change His mind.

God is not human, that he should lie, not a human being, that he should change his mind. Does he speak and then not act? Does he promise and not fulfill? (Numbers 23:19)

The implicit message of Jonah 3 could be that God changed His mind. The explicit statement of Numbers 23 is that God does not change His mind. From this we should understand that in Jonah 3, God made a threat, but that the threat was conditional. The whole point of Jonah going to Nineveh was to bring a message that would produce repentance. After all, if God had made a final determination to destroy Nineveh, there would be no reason to send Jonah to them.

Sometimes it is hard to recognize that some part of Scripture is implicit, especially if we bring our own expectations to the text. If we have always understood a passage a certain way, we may not even see that what we view as an explicit statement is, in fact, a statement that implies something, from which we make what appears to be a natural inference. Sometimes we value that inference because it supports a theological position we hold. Sadly, we don't even see that we are interpreting the passage by making assumptions.

Some passages contain a certain level of subtlety that requires us to really pay attention to the details in the text. Our biggest obstacle, however, is what we cannot see because we think we already know what the text says and what it means.

THEOLOGICAL BARRIERS TO SEEING THE TEXT

It is important to understand the theology of the Bible. But our theological point of view must be subservient to what God's Word says. There are times when someone holds a theological position that can be discredited by the biblical text. Yet they may continue to hold that position because it is so integral to what they believe that they simply cannot change their mind. We might think this is a problem with new seminary students, and perhaps it is. But it is even more of a problem for experienced pastors and seminary professors. If the thing they have taught for years is not true, it might discredit the work they have done. As a result, they will argue for a position that requires assumptions that appear to be unfounded.

This might seem like a bold claim. Perhaps it is. But suppose we look at a section of Scripture that is foundational to Christian theology. Let's consider Genesis 1–3 and think about whether the things we have always believed are supported by or denied by Scripture.

06

INTERPRETING GENESIS 1—3

The account of creation and the fall is critically important because it forms the foundation for how we understand a variety of theological issues. Yet the different interpretations of the first three chapters of Genesis are almost too many to count. When reading this part of Scripture, we're often hindered by the theology filter—which interprets the text through our own theological views—and by the experience filter, which tempts us to see what we want to see in the text.

In recent years, many Christians have espoused a view of the creation account that simply denies that the biblical account is historical or real. Even believers who say they believe in the Bible as the Word of God will sometimes deny the reality of the tempting of Adam and the Woman.

Some people object to the creation account because they believe in evolution. Others reject it because it contains talking animals or because it seems too harsh for God to condemn all of humanity for eating a piece of fruit.

There is a problem, however, with denying the fall that is described in Genesis. If humanity did not fall by disobeying God's command not to eat the fruit, we have to provide another explanation for why everyone sins. Do we sin because God didn't want to make humanity good? Do we sin because God was unable to make humanity good? Was God uninvolved in making man and if so, does that mean humanity is not made in the image of God?

A Christian view of the world would appear to require that man is made in God's image and that God, who is called a creator in various parts of Scripture, must have made the world and humanity. If God made humanity, it is only reasonable that a Holy God would have made sinless people.

If we theorize that the Genesis account is not an accurate presentation of how humanity came into existence, we quickly run into problems. In the discussion that follows, I will assume the accuracy and historicity of the account of the creation of the world and humanity in Genesis 1-3.

Before we start, think about what you know about the creation of Adam and the Woman. Most Christians know what they believe about the creation story. If our views are already firmly established, we probably know everything that is in the text. If we know the text really well, we may feel confident there is nothing new for us to see.

BUT SUPPOSE THERE WAS SOMETHING YOU HADN'T SEEN BEFORE?

You have probably heard the debate about whether the days of creation are single literal days or if they are perhaps very long periods of undetermined length. The second view is often held by people who support theistic evolution (evolution guided by God). You almost certainly have an opinion about which day of creation God made Adam and the Woman. If you hold to theistic evolution, it may seem to be an irrelevant question.

This section of Scripture allows us to practice using many of the tools presented in this book. In Genesis 1-3, we need to use CLAP, Scripture interprets Scripture, interpreting the implicit by the explicit, and allowing Scripture to determine theology rather than giving theology the final word on what we believe.

THE DAYS OF CREATION

Let's begin by reading portions of the text in Genesis 1.

> And God said, "Let the earth sprout vegetation, plants yielding seed, and fruit trees bearing fruit in which is their seed, each according to its kind, on the earth." And it was so. The earth brought forth vegetation, plants yielding seed according to their own kinds, and trees bearing fruit in which is their seed, each according to its kind. And God saw that it was good. And there was evening and there was morning, the third day. (Genesis 1:11–13 ESV)

IN THESE PASSAGES IN GENESIS, ON WHAT DAY ARE ALL THE PLANTS CREATED BY GOD?

I am tempted to ask this question several times and have you answer it as often as I ask it, just to reinforce the clarity of this passage. It seems clear that all vegetation, plants, and trees were made on the third day. This appears to cover every kind of horticulture.

IS THERE ANY KIND OF PLANT EXCLUDED FROM THE CREATION ACCOUNT OF THE THIRD DAY OF CREATION?

The text says that vegetation, plants yielding seed, and fruit trees bearing fruit were made on the third day. That seems to cover all horticulture. We will see the significance of this shortly.

> Then God said, "Let us make man in our image, after our likeness. And let them have dominion over the fish of the sea and over the birds of the heavens and over the livestock and over all the earth and over every creeping thing that creeps on the earth."
> So God created man in his own image, in the image of God he created him; male and female he created them.
> And God saw everything that he had made, and behold, it was very good. And there was evening and there was morning, the sixth day. (Genesis 1:26–27, 31 ESV)

DOES THE GENESIS 1:26—27 PASSAGE EXPLICITLY OR IMPLICITLY STATE THAT ADAM AND THE WOMAN WERE MADE ON THE SIXTH DAY?

The answer to this question is not clear. If you read the Genesis passage carefully, the points made in the text are that on the sixth day God made man in His image, He gave humanity dominion over all the earth, and He made man male and female.

There are two elements in this passage that are explicit: first, God made man in His image. The humans became image bearers on the sixth day. Second, God made humanity male and female on the sixth day. Neither of these explicit statements actually say that God physically made Adam and the Woman on the sixth day. An explicit statement in the text would say, "God made the man and woman on the sixth day." But what does the text actually say? "God created man in his own image, in the image of God he created him; male and female he created them" (v. 27).

If we compare the language of the sixth day with the third day, there is a difference. The language about creating the vegetation is explicit. God said, "Let the earth sprout vegetation and the earth brought forth vegetation."

The explicit statements about humanity on the sixth day emphasize God making/creating, but that making and creating is focused on image bearing and gender. Now you might think that God making man in His image on the sixth day is the same as saying God physically created Adam and the Woman's bodies on the sixth day. That is a natural implication, but the two things may or may not be identical. In the absence of any other information, we would accept that Adam and the Woman were physically created on the sixth day. Likewise, you might think the phrase "male and female He created them" means that God made both genders on the sixth day. It appears to be a natural inference that God making humanity male and female is equal to God making both Adam and the Woman on the sixth day. However, the making of the humans on the sixth day is implied, not stated explicitly.

The challenge for us is to put aside what we think we already know and consider whether the statements about image bearing and gender are identical to physical creation. They may be, or we may be injecting an element of interpretation. We might argue that everyone agrees that this is what the text means. That does not make it true. If we are interpreting or assuming certain things, we may find that what we have always known is not true at all.

From Genesis 1, we have the strong implication that both the Woman and the man were made on the sixth day. Oh, and by the way, we cannot call the Woman Eve at this point, because she only becomes Eve after the fall.

Now we come to Genesis 2. Some suggest that there are two creation stories and that they argue with each other. But if the Bible is the Word of God, inspired by the Holy Spirit, no two passages will teach something mutually incompatible. The Bible is God-breathed, and is useful for teaching, rebuking, correcting, and training in righteousness (2 Tim. 3:16). It is coherent and consistent; God does not contradict Himself in the biblical text. This means that Genesis 2 cannot disagree with Genesis 1. The content of Genesis 2 is consistent with what is taught in Genesis 1.

Most people have already concluded that Adam and the Woman are physically created on the sixth day based on the strong implication in Genesis 1. That conclusion prevents us from paying attention to the clear teaching in Genesis 2.

> Now the LORD God had *formed out of the ground all the wild animals and all the birds in the sky.* He brought them to the man to see what he would name them; and whatever the man called each living creature, that was its name. So *the man gave names to all the livestock, the birds in the sky and all the wild animals.*
>
> But for Adam no suitable helper was found. So the LORD God caused the man to fall into a deep sleep; and while he was sleeping, he took one of the man's ribs and then closed up the place with flesh. *Then the LORD God made a woman from the rib he had taken out of the man, and he brought her to the man.*
>
> The man said, "This is now bone of my bones and flesh of my flesh; she shall be called woman, for she was taken out of man." (Genesis 2:19–23, *emphasis added*)

ON WHAT DAY ARE THE BIRDS MADE? ON WHAT DAY ARE THE ANIMALS MADE? BASED ON THAT, IS IT EXPLICIT OR IMPLICIT THAT THE WOMAN WAS MADE ON THE SIXTH DAY?

It is clear that the Woman is made on the sixth day. What is implied in chapter 1 is stated explicitly in chapter 2: the Woman was physically made after the animals. The birds and the animals are created on the sixth day.

GOING ON, DOES GENESIS 2 TELL US EXPLICITLY OR IMPLICITLY THAT ADAM WAS MADE ON THE SIXTH DAY?

Let's read the account of Adam's creation.

> *When no bush of the field was yet in the land and no small plant of the field had yet sprung up*—for the LORD God had *not caused it to rain* on the land, and there was *no man to work the ground,* and a mist was going up from the land and was watering the whole face of the ground—then the LORD God formed the man of dust from the ground and breathed into his nostrils the breath of life, and the man became a living creature. And the LORD God planted a garden in Eden, in the east, and there he put the man whom he had formed. And out of the ground *the LORD God made to spring up every tree that is pleasant to the sight and good for food.* The tree of life was in the midst of the garden, and the tree of the knowledge of good and evil. (Genesis 2:5-9 ESV, *emphasis added*)

Now this is a trick question. Genesis 2 does *not* explicitly say that Adam was created on the sixth day. It also does *not* implicitly say that he was created on the sixth day.

06: INTERPRETING GENESIS 1—3

BASED ON THE EXPLICIT INFORMATION IN THE GENESIS 2 AND THE EXPLICIT INFORMATION IN GENESIS 1:9—13, ON WHAT DAY OF THE WEEK OF CREATION WAS ADAM MADE?

This can be confusing. Genesis 1 seems to imply that Adam and the Woman were both made on the sixth day. When we start with chapter 1, we make certain assumptions. Because humanity, male and female, are made on the sixth day, almost everyone has treated Genesis 1 as an explicit text. But with a careful reading, we see that it does not literally say that Adam and the Woman were created on the sixth day.[1]

If we have already decided that Adam was made on the sixth day, when we come to Genesis 2, we don't pay attention to its explicit statements. If we ignore the details of chapter 2 and assume that chapter 1 has answered the question, we miss the substance of Genesis' teaching about the creation of Adam.

To be clear, Genesis 2 also does not explicitly say that Adam was made on the third day. But if we look at the details, Genesis 2 does explicitly state that Adam was physically made before the vegetation was formed. Consider the details provided in Genesis 2:5: "when no plant of the field was yet in the earth and no herb of the field had yet sprung up—for the LORD God had not caused it to rain upon the earth, and there was no one to till the ground." Let's think about what the Genesis 2 passage says. It explicitly states that no bush or small plant had sprung up. Why? No rain and no man. If Adam was made on the sixth day and it rained on the third day, would there have been bushes and small plants on the third day? I think we have to say no, because Genesis 2 gives two reasons that no small plant of the field had yet sprung up. No man would have meant no small plants.

---

1 Very different Hebrew words are used in Genesis 1 and 2 to describe God making and creating. When God makes Adam, the text uses the word *formed*. When God makes the Woman out of Adam's rib, the text uses a different word that means *to build*. The Hebrew word used in Genesis 1:26 "Let us make man..." is a word that means *make*, but it is often used to describe making something out of something else (see Isaiah 44:15, 17 where the same word is used). The implication could be that the image bearing resulted from an imposition of God's image on our first parents. In Genesis 1:27, "So God created man in his own image, in the image of God he created him; male and female he created them," the same word create is used as was found in Genesis 1:1. This threefold create, focuses on the image of God and on male and female gender, using different language than the subsequent description of physical making.

Now you may be tempted to try and explain this away, which is what we often do when a passage in Scripture doesn't fit our preconceptions. You may wonder, for example, if the plants made after the man—the bushes and the small plants of the field—were different than the plants created on the third day. What if God created all plants on the third day, except for crops that need cultivation and watering? Maybe those plants were created after the man?

That theory might appear to solve the problem of the need for rain and a man to work the soil. But there are problems with this interpretation.

- Did the creation of horticulture on the third day include all plants except those that were useful for food? (Genesis 1 gives the impression that all plants were made on the third day, not just a subset of vegetation that didn't need rain or cultivation.)
- If these crops were made after Adam, when were they made? (We have no record of a subsequent making of additional plants in the biblical account.)
- Did the plants created on the third day—supposedly before Adam—not need rain?
- How does this theory account for plants that are more dependent on rain than grains and vegetables?
- Aren't crops plants that yield seed and fruit trees that bear fruit? If so, aren't they exactly what is being described in Genesis 1:11? "And God said, 'Let the earth sprout vegetation, plants yielding seed, and fruit trees bearing fruit in which is their seed, each according to its kind, on the earth.'"[2]

2 There are many ways that commentators explain Adam's creation in Genesis 2 that precedes creation of the plants. Some say that the plants that followed Adam's creation were crops. Others say that the seeds were in the ground awaiting rain and creation of the man. The idea has been proposed that the vegetation of the third day was growing, but there was no garden that required rain or man to cultivate it. All of these require significant assumptions that cannot be justified in the text. In Genesis 1:11-13 God says let the plants sprout, so they are not seeds. Also, as stated above, the plants bear seeds and the trees bear fruit, which is the very essence of what makes up crops. There are few crops that don't bear seeds as described in Genesis 1 (all grains, all nuts, most if not all tubers, and all fruits fit the description in Genesis 1). As you read through this section, it is helpful to keep in mind a couple of points. The same Hebrew words are used of the plants in Genesis 1:11 and 2:5. Additionally, there is no indication in Scripture that the creation of plants in Genesis 1 was incomplete. The language is similar to that accompanying the creation of the birds, fish, and animals.

It is interesting that the same word that means "green plants" is used in the Hebrew text in Genesis 1:11 and in Genesis 2:5. The Septuagint also uses the same Greek word (*chorton*) to describe the green plants in Genesis 1:11 and in Genesis 2:5. The biblical author did not distinguish between the two types of plants.

So it appears that the plants were not made on two separate occasions, but that all the plants were made on the third day. After all, the fish and the birds were made on the fifth day and there is no indication some were made one day and others on another. The beasts and creeping things were all made on the sixth day with no indication that God added to their number later.

What is explicit from Genesis 2 is that Adam was made before the plants sprung up, and Genesis 1 explicitly states that God made vegetation on the third day of creation.

THIS RAISES THE QUESTION: HOW ARE WE TO UNDERSTAND CHAPTER 1 AND THE SIXTH DAY?

We begin by applying the CLAP principles. We pay attention to the details presented in what is implicit. The text says God made humanity in His image and that He made them male *and* female on the sixth day. We also note that in Genesis 1 the animals were made on the sixth day. Now we go back to Genesis 2 and we see that God stated that it was not good for man to be alone. Then God formed the animals; after that, He made the Woman from Adam's rib. Obviously, this had to happen on the sixth day since that was when the animals were made. This helps us see that on the sixth day humanity was made in God's image, male and female, and not before the sixth day, because prior to the sixth day there was no human female image bearer.

WHAT DOES THIS SUGGEST ABOUT THE SIGNIFICANCE OF GENDER?

It appears God gives us our gender (Ps. 139:13, Jer. 1:5), and connects our value, as those made in the image of God, to our gender in the creation account. And that value exists whether we are male or female. This assigns value to us as gendered people. The image of God is not found exclusively in a male image bearer. Both genders together bear God's image.

This clarifies that the image of God is not merely the male, father image that we naturally recognize from the language of Scripture. The image of God is male *and* female. This suggests that we need each other, because it is humanity in both genders that expresses the fullness of the image of God. We are individually image bearers. But in our diverse roles as male and female we represent God's image more completely. This should not be surprising, because God describes Himself as a father but also uses language that fits the female role.

> For this is what the LORD *says:* "I will extend peace to her like a river, and the wealth of nations like a flooding stream; you will nurse and be carried on her arm and dandled on her knees. *As a mother comforts her child, so will I comfort you*; and you will be comforted over Jerusalem." (Isaiah 66:12–13, *emphasis added*)

> You deserted the Rock, who *fathered you*; you forgot the God who *gave you birth*. The LORD *saw this and rejected them* because he was angered by his sons and daughters. "I will hide my face from them," he said, "and see what their end will be; for they are a perverse generation, children who are unfaithful. (Deuteronomy 32:18–20, *emphasis added*)

This calls us to recognize the image of God in both genders. If we value all image bearers, our treatment of all people will reflect the respect, kindness, and honor we owe to those made in God's image. This has implications for gender, race, and health/disability issues.

INTERESTINGLY, IF ADAM WAS MADE ON THE THIRD DAY AND THE WOMAN WAS MADE ON THE SIXTH DAY, WHAT ARE THE IMPLICATIONS FOR THEISTIC EVOLUTION?

If Adam was created on the third day and the Woman was made on the sixth day, we can no longer propose theistic evolution. If it was not good for Adam to be alone, it would not make sense for God to make Adam wait hundreds, thousands, or millions of years before providing the Woman who

06: INTERPRETING GENESIS 1–3

would fill up what was lacking for Adam. The days of creation might not have been exactly twenty-four hours long, but they would have been short enough that Adam would not be alone for an excessive period.

WHAT ELSE DOES ALL THIS TEACH US?

Genesis 1–3 raises all kinds of problems for our typical interpretation of creation and the fall. There are a lot of difficult questions:

- Why did the Woman eat the fruit?
- Did Adam observe that the Woman was fallen before he ate the fruit?
- What was Adam's motivation to eat the fruit?
- How can it be appropriate to speak of Jesus as the Second Adam? Isn't Jesus so far above Adam that there is no comparison?
- What is meant by "your desire will be for your husband" (Gen. 3:16)?
- Is "your husband will rule over you" a curse or a restatement of what already existed?
- Do we view Adam and the Woman before the fall as being like us, or are they totally different from us because they are made without sin?
- Why don't we fall in the Woman if she ate the fruit first?

We can't cover all these questions in detail, but perhaps we can say a few things about some of them. In some cases, we may be able to make statements about what we know is true. We may be able to say that what we have always known is not true. Perhaps we can at least offer some clarification and point those who want to explore this further in the right direction.

Some of what I will point out will run squarely into the theological filters I mentioned in the introduction to this chapter. If you are familiar with systematic theology textbooks and commentaries on Genesis, you likely recognize that they generally speak about the first three chapters of Genesis with one voice. You will also see that I present information that contradicts what they say. The question is, does the biblical text support the position held by many of those scholarly works, or does the Bible present a different view?

And if the Bible does present a different view, will you prioritize what the scholars teach over what the Bible says?

Let's start with a pretty clear example. Many theology books and commentaries consistently say the Woman was motivated to eat the fruit because she was proud, felt God was withholding good from her, or that she wanted to displace God. But there is a problem. All of these theories require the Woman to be sinful before she ate the fruit.

IS THAT A PROBLEM?

The Bible is clear that the Woman became a sinner by eating the fruit.

> And Adam was not the one deceived; it was the woman who was deceived and became a sinner. (1 Timothy 2:14)

Paul clearly alludes to the Woman being deceived by the serpent. Her action, having been deceived, was to eat the fruit. That is what caused her to become a sinner. By implication, that tells us that she was not a sinner before she ate the fruit.

What is sin? It is evil, expressed in many ways. We can summarize it in our lives as evil deeds, evil words, evil thoughts, evil motivations, and evil attitudes. Now suppose the Woman was proud. Is that not a sin? But if she was sinful for even one second before she ate the fruit, she did not become a sinner by eating the fruit! Suppose the Woman wanted to displace God. We would either have to attribute that to megalomania (mental illness) or a sinful attitude of hostility toward God. In either case, we would have to believe that she was broken and sinful before she ate the fruit. In such a case, she would not be good. Yet God said everything He made was good.

> God saw all that he had made, and it was very good. And there was evening, and there was morning—the sixth day. (Genesis 1:31)

The same would be true if the Woman felt God was withholding good from her. Such a thought would be sinful but would occur before she ate the fruit. None of these explanations of the Woman's motives in eating the fruit are reasonable. All of them require the Woman to be sinful before she fell.

These explanations view the Woman as being just like us, fallen and sinful, *before she ate the fruit*. But she was not like us. She had to be without sin when she was deceived, or she could not have become a sinner when she was deceived.

Many of our ideas about Adam and the Woman are corrupted by our natural condition. Because sinful thoughts, words, deeds, motivations, and attitudes are normal and unavoidable for us, we find it difficult to imagine what it was like for our first parents to be without sin before they ate the fruit. This could be why our theology books ascribe motives to the Woman that would require her to be sinful before she ate the fruit. However, the Scriptures do not allow us to hold that position.

In Adam, we observe may of the same problems—and more. His motivations and thoughts were also sinless, right up to the moment he ate the fruit. If we ascribe sinful motives to him, such as pride, we make Adam like us. But if he was sinful before the fall, then our fall would not be due to his eating the fruit but to some other cause.

For a more detailed explanation of Adam and the Woman's motivations, read *The Beginning: A Second Look at the First Sin*, from Square Halo Books.

DID ADAM RECOGNIZE THAT THE WOMAN HAD BECOME SINFUL?

David described his sin as impacting him as though his bones were crushed.

> Let me hear joy and gladness;
> let the bones you have crushed rejoice. (Psalm 51:8)

Or consider how God's punishment of sin is described in Isaiah:

> Surely he took up our pain and bore our suffering, yet we considered him punished by God, stricken by him, and afflicted. But he was pierced for our transgressions, he was crushed for our iniquities; the

punishment that brought us peace was on him, and by his wounds we are healed. (Isaiah 53:4-5)

David was like us—he was an experienced sinner. Yet he describes the impact of sin on him as so severe that it was like having his bones crushed. And Isaiah's description of the impact of our sins on Jesus, and the punishment He had to face to free us from them, shows how serious sin is.

Have you ever been so struck by the recognition of your own sin that you felt like weeping or even felt physically sick because of your guilt? Now how would you expect a person to react who was without sin—no guilt, no shame, no regrets of past sins—after she committed her first sin? Suddenly she knew guilt, she knew shame, and she had become fully sinful. Her thoughts, attitudes, motivations, words, and deeds had been corrupted. For the first time she was alienated from God, her husband, and all creation.

Let's pause a moment, because I want you to think about what we are doing here as we interpret the Bible. Some of this is Scripture interprets Scripture. But some of this is simply taking the text seriously. The text doesn't say how the Woman reacted. So how can we say anything that isn't pure speculation about the Woman's reaction to eating the fruit?

We know sin well. We know its corrosive impact on us, and how we feel when we sin, and when our sins are exposed. We can look at the verses above and at our own experience to help us understand the effect sin might have had on the Woman. Our sins required the perfect Son of Man to be tortured to death over many hours. So, unless we have a very low view of sin, we should expect the Woman to be very adversely impacted by her sin. She would have been more severely impacted than anything we have ever experienced.

I would be shocked if the Woman was not physically sick and weeping uncontrollably after she ate the fruit. It is only because we are practiced and sophisticated sinners, who sin with style and grace, that we don't recognize the impact of the first sin on the Woman. It appears inevitable that sinless Adam would have recognized how sin affected the Woman.

As the Woman was sinless, so was Adam. We don't have time to explore all the details related to Adam. But there are a couple of points that may clarify things for us. While nothing sinful affected Adam's decision to eat the fruit, that does not mean he made a good decision. People with good intentions often make bad decisions.

First Timothy 2:14 says that Adam was not the one deceived. If he thought anything good would come from eating the fruit, he would have been deceived. But if Adam was not deceived, he had to know that eating the fruit would harm him.

FEDERAL HEADSHIP

For an excellent example of how applying a theological filter can affect our ability to interpret Scripture, let's look at the concept of Federal Headship,[3] which proposes that Adam was the federal head over all creation and that we could only fall through his disobedience. The idea of a pre-fall human hierarchy (where one person serves as a federal head) is found nowhere in Scripture, but some things are stated explicitly.

- Humans fell through the sin of Adam.
- Therefore, just as sin entered the world through one man, and death through sin, and in this way death came to all people, because all sinned. To be sure, sin was in the world before the law was given, but sin is not charged against anyone's account where there is no law. Nevertheless, death reigned from the time of Adam to the time of Moses, even over those who did not *sin by breaking a command, as did Adam*, who is a pattern of the one to come. (Romans 5:12–14, emphasis added)
- The Woman fell before Adam.
- Adam was formed first, giving him some sort of priority.
- The Woman was deceived, leading to her becoming a sinner, but Adam was not deceived.

3 For an explanation of Federal Headship see: *What is meant by federal headship? What is the concept of federal headship?* at CompellingTruth.org or *What is the meaning of federal headship?* at GotQuestions.org

- A woman should learn in quietness and full submission. I do not permit a woman to teach or to assume authority over a man; she must be quiet. For Adam was formed first, then Eve. And Adam was *not the one deceived*; it was *the woman* who *was deceived and became a sinner.* (1 Timothy 2:11–14, *emphasis added*)

The primary issue is that the Woman sinned first, before Adam, yet we fall in Adam. Federal Headship solves this problem by saying that Adam was made first and so had priority that made him the federal head over creation. In this view, the Woman could do anything, and her actions would have no effect on the rest of humanity. But when Adam sinned, everyone was corrupted and fallen because he represented us as the federal head.

Romans 5:12–21 clearly states that humanity fell through Adam. However, nowhere is the concept that Adam served as a federal head for humanity found in the creation account or anywhere else in Scripture. There are passages that talk about male authority in the church and the marriage relationship, but all of them are focused on the post-fall condition.

The major problem with Federal Headship is that it requires huge assumptions. It forces us to accept that Adam being made first means that "Adam was constituted the representative head of the human race, so that he could act for all his descendants."[4] That idea has absolutely no biblical support.

We can agree that Adam has a priority by being formed first. That is, after all, the point Paul is making in 1 Timothy 2. But the real question is, what is the significance of that priority? There are a couple of options:

- Adam could be designated by God as the head of the human race.
- Adam could have priority comparable to a professor emeritus.

If Adam's priority as the head of the human race was such that he alone represented humanity in the temptation, Paul could have made a simple point. He could have said that Adam had priority by being formed first, and nothing further would need to be said. Paul's point that women are to learn in

---

4   Louis Berkhof, *Systematic Theology,* 4th Edition (Grand Rapids, MI: Eerdmans, 1977, orig. pub. 1939), 215.

full submission would be complete simply by pointing to Adam's primacy.[5]

But Paul's argument is not complete! When Paul notes that the Woman was deceived, he is telling us that Adam's priority, in having been made first, is not sufficient to justify women's submission. This alone discredits the idea of pre-fall Adam as head of the human race.

SO WHY DOES IT MATTER THAT THE WOMAN WAS DECEIVED AND BECAME A SINNER?

The significance of the Woman being deceived is that the decision she made to eat the fruit was not a choice to rebel against God. It appears that the Woman's sin did not impact all humanity and all creation because it was not characteristic of most human sin which is rebellion against God.

Paul uses the curse God places upon the Woman after the fall to justify the submission Paul describes in 1 Timothy 2. There is a pattern of two curses for each participant in the fall: the serpent will crawl on his belly and will experience enmity with the Woman, culminating in her offspring crushing the serpent's offspring. The Woman will have pain in childbirth, and (as clarified by the Septuagint - LXX) her hostility (not desire) will be toward her husband—he will rule over her. Work, for Adam, will be painful toil and he will eventually die (Gen. 3:14–19).

All these things are changes of status. If Adam already ruled over the Woman, her second curse would be meaningless. This presents Adam's priority at creation as something like that of a professor emeritus. He is older and more experienced (having seen most of God's creative work), but he is not a supervisor, boss, or ruler.

We should distinguish between a hierarchy of God over humanity and a hierarchy of humans over humans. Human authorities exist in a fallen reality because they maintain peace and order.

---

5   I should note here that the submission described in Scripture is not the harsh male domination that is sometimes improperly justified by the use of these passages. A careful discussion of the issue can be found in the last chapter of, *The Beginning: A Second Look at the First Sin,* by A.D. Bauer.

> I urge, then, first of all, that petitions, prayers, intercession and thanksgiving be made for all people—for kings and all those in authority, that we may live peaceful and quiet lives in all godliness and holiness. (1 Timothy 2:1–2)

WOULD THERE BE A NEED FOR A PRE-FALL HIERARCHY IF BOTH PEOPLE WERE UNFALLEN?

Peace and order naturally exist when all humans are without sin. Think about what life would be like if you lived among sinless humans. If the person in front of you never sinned, he would not lie to you, steal from you, act violently toward you, or commit any other sin against you. Rather, a sinless person would act in a loving way, emulating Christ, who never sinned, and he would look for ways to do good to you. It would come naturally for that sinless person to sacrifice for you. And if you were without sin, you would act in the same way toward him. There would therefore be no need for anyone to be in charge.

But once sin entered the world, someone had to be in charge to maintain peace and order. The cursing of the Woman imposed a hierarchy and established something that had not previously existed, suggesting there was no hierarchy before the fall.

SO WHY DO WE FALL IN ADAM AND NOT THE WOMAN?

As described above, the Woman was deceived (Gen. 3:13, 2 Cor. 11:3, 1 Tim. 2:14) and convinced to eat. Her act is not a decision to disobey God. So, we do not fall in the Woman. We fall in Adam because he was not deceived (1 Tim. 2:14). Adam ate the fruit knowing that he was disobeying God. And because he was not deceived, he ate knowing that eating the fruit would harm him. Again, if you want a fuller explanation, read *The Beginning: A Second Look at the First Sin*.

This close study of Genesis 1–3 shows us how easy it is to miss the meaning of a biblical passage when we either overlook what is in the passage or assume the presence of something that is not. By applying tools like CLAP or Scripture interprets Scripture, we're able to see God's Word more clearly. In the next chapter, we'll put these skills to further use as we explore the text of Revelation.

07

INTERPRETING REVELATION

When I studied eschatology (end times) in seminary, I read thousands of pages and came away without a clear view of how to understand Revelation. So I am thankful to Dr. Gordon Fee for teaching me that the key to interpreting this biblical book lies in understanding the meaning of the images. I eventually pursued this line of research and through Square Halo Books published *The End: A Reader's Guide to Revelation.* In that book, I included a glossary that provides definitions for many of the images.

Before we go further in our discussion, we should think about our expectations for eschatological material. Many people have missed a proper interpretation of the biblical text because they brought expectations to the text that did not match the teaching of Scripture. Those miscues fall into several categories.

I HOLD THE ONLY BIBLICAL VIEW OF CHRIST'S RETURN

This is the classic example of the tail wagging the dog. Eschatological passages are often filled with imagery and are inherently difficult to interpret. Yet there is no part of theology where we see more dogmatism. As I said earlier, every major position related to end times has difficulties. The strongest proponents of each position spend much of their time *explaining away* objections to their view. In such a complex area of theology, common sense would seem to dictate that we approach the task of interpretation carefully. The proper method should involve the following:

- Start with *no* eschatological position and look to see what the biblical text teaches on the subject. I know that is difficult for those who have a hard and fast theological framework. But Scripture is more important than our position, and only Scripture can cure the blindness we all bring to this issue.
- Listen to each other humbly and recognize that our goal is to understand what to expect regarding the return of Christ.
- Avoid trying to "win" the argument with the image bearing believers with whom you discuss the issue. Do you care more about that dear brother or sister or about winning?

LOOKING FOR THE ANTICHRIST

If you search the Internet, you will find writers who identify the antichrist as Prince Charles, Bill Gates, the current pope, and any number of other people. Often this is done by using gimmicks to manipulate gematria (a form of interpretation that replaces letters with numbers based on a formula of a=1, b=2, etc.). It appears that people want these public figures to be the antichrist and so twist interpretative techniques to reach their goal. But because these writers do not use the Scriptures to determine which characteristics the antichrist will have, they consistently miss their goal.

NOW IS THE TIME OF THE END

Martin Luther stated that he was sure he was living in the last days, because things were so bad he was confident the Lord was coming back very soon. Of course, that was hundreds of years ago, and the Lord did not come back in Luther's time. Yet many hold the same view today. Scripture contains several criteria that indicate when the Lord will come back. None of them are "Things are so bad the Lord must be coming back soon."

07: INTERPRETING REVELATION

THAT LOOKS JUST LIKE . . .

One of the worst interpretive approaches to Revelation and eschatology involves judging the meaning of imagery using the "that looks just like" method. As an example, let's look at the mark of the beast. The image of a mark has been taken literally as a physical pattern, which has led some people to equate the mark with a tattoo or a bar code. People say, "That part of Revelation looks just like a tattoo of a number." But as things change, they say, "That part of Revelation looks just like a bar code." As culture and technology continue to change, they say, "That looks just like a microchip." But Scripture says it is none of those things. If these readers looked more closely at the Scriptures than they do at their own preconceived notions, they would recognize that.

> This observance *will be for you like a sign on your hand and a reminder on your forehead* that this law of the Lord is to be on your lips. For the Lord brought you out of Egypt with his mighty hand. You must keep this ordinance at the appointed time year after year. (Exodus 13:9–10, *emphasis added*)
>
> "When Pharaoh stubbornly refused to let us go, the Lord killed the firstborn of both people and animals in Egypt. This is why I sacrifice to the Lord the first male offspring of every womb and redeem each of my firstborn sons." And *it will be like a sign on your hand and a symbol on your forehead* that the Lord brought us out of Egypt with his mighty hand. (Exodus 13:15–16, *emphasis added*)

The sign on the hand and symbol on the forehead in Exodus is not a physical mark but a practice, Passover, that sets Israelites apart. When the antichrist establishes a mark (on the hand or on the forehead) it should be expected, following the biblical language, to be a practice. Marks on the hand or forehead are distinct in that they appear on parts of the body that are normally visible to everyone. Passover was described as a marking of hand and forehead, because it was a practice that was visible and would be recognized as something that set Jews apart from others.

The "that looks just like" interpretive approach results in Scriptural interpretations that change as culture and technology changes. It also leads to interpretations that would have been meaningless to first-century Christians. When we apply the Scripture interprets Scripture approach to studying the mark of beast, we can see that the mark is not a tattoo, bar code, or a microchip, because those interpretations are not consistent with anything we see elsewhere in Scripture.

AWAITING THE THIRD COMING

There are many different ways to interpret eschatological material, but one thing that has been done and that cannot be justified is proposing a third coming of Christ. We believe that Christ came as a child in the first coming, and we believe that Jesus will return in His second coming. However, some preterists propose that Jesus already came a second time and will come a third time. Likewise, some premillennialists propose that Jesus will come in a secret rapture second coming and then will return a third time. The difficulties with these positions abound. Preterists say Jesus came in 70 AD and no one actually saw him. Premillennialists say Jesus will come secretly, and no one will see His second coming except those who disappear.

Compare both these views with the language of Scripture that describes a visible return of Christ.

When Christ ascended, He went up into the sky until He was hidden from His disciples' eyes by a cloud. Just before this happened, Jesus spoke to His disciples.

> "But you will receive power when the Holy Spirit comes on you; and you will be my witnesses in Jerusalem, and in all Judea and Samaria, and to the ends of the earth."
>
> After he said this, *he was taken up before their very eyes, and a cloud hid him from their sight.*
>
> They were looking intently up into the sky as he was going, when suddenly two men dressed in white stood beside them. "Men of

07: INTERPRETING REVELATION

Galilee," they said, "why do you stand here looking into the sky? This same Jesus, who has been taken from you into heaven, *will come back in the same way you have seen him go into heaven.*" (Acts 1:8-11, *emphasis added*)

Several texts also speak of the return (singular) of Christ as being announced by a trumpet call and as being visible as lightening that shines from the East to the West. Any view that proposes an invisible return of Christ contradicts these descriptions in the Gospels, Acts, and Paul. Such a view denies that Jesus will come back in the same way the disciples saw Him go.

Any view that proposes that Christ returns twice also denies the clear teaching of Scripture, since Paul suggests that he and the recipients of his letters were waiting for the loud and visible return of Christ.

> Concerning the coming of our Lord Jesus Christ and our being gathered to him, we ask you, brothers and sisters, not to become easily unsettled or alarmed by the teaching allegedly from us—whether by a prophecy or by word of mouth or by letter—asserting that the day of the Lord has already come. Don't let anyone deceive you in any way, for *that day will not come until the rebellion occurs and the man of lawlessness is revealed*, the man doomed to destruction. (2 Thessalonians 2:1-3, *emphasis added*)

> According to the Lord's word, we tell you that *we who are still alive*, who are left until the coming of the Lord, will certainly not precede those who have fallen asleep. For the Lord himself will come down from heaven, *with a loud command*, with *the voice of the archangel* and with *the trumpet call of God*, and the dead in Christ will rise first. After that, *we who are still alive* and are left will be caught up together with them in the clouds to meet the Lord in the air. And so *we* will be with the Lord forever. Therefore *encourage one another with these words.* (1 Thessalonians 4:15-18, *emphasis added*)

As you read these passages from Paul you should note a couple of things. The Lord will not come until the antichrist is revealed (2 Thess. 2:3). This makes an invisible return of Christ before the antichrist appears impossible. Also, the return Paul is anticipating, potentially for himself and for the people to whom he is writing, involves a loud command, the voice of the archangel, and the trumpet call of God (1 Thess. 4:16). The entire point of these things is that they are loud and noisy. And Paul says "we" who are still alive will be caught up in the clouds, and that the recipients of his letter should encourage each other (1 Thess. 4:17–18), *because this is, based on the inspired Word of God, the return the first-century Christians were all expecting!* It should also be noticed that Paul says "we" will be with the Lord *forever* (1 Thess. 4:17), denying that there is another subsequent return.

These texts describe features that did not happen in 70 AD. There was no visible and noisy return that could be seen from the East to the West. There were no living people caught up with the dead, meeting the Lord—who had come back in the way the disciples saw Him go, as described in the book of Acts—in the air.

It is interesting that the idea of a third coming is almost never discussed by those holding views that require Christ to come a third time. All the imagery and the various features of the alternate positions so muddy the waters, that many proponents of "third coming" eschatological views don't even realize that their position requires a third coming. Even when they do recognize this, they are often so devoted to their theology that they attempt to explain away the Scriptures. Their theological filters remain firmly in place as theology overcomes the biblical text.

07: INTERPRETING REVELATION

SO WHAT ARE THE SIGNS OF THE END?

The Scriptures do tell us some things about when Christ will return. We can't predict the day and hour of Christ's return, but we can see what we have been told about it.

THE GOSPEL

The first sign that Christ is going to return soon is that the gospel will be proclaimed throughout the world.

> And this gospel of the kingdom will be preached in the whole world as a testimony to all nations, and then the end will come. (Matthew 24:14)

LAWLESSNESS

The second sign of the return of Christ is the growth in lawlessness and the love of most growing cold. This is different than saying that things are so bad that Christ must return soon. Lawlessness refers both to people breaking the law and to the failure of authority to rein in the lawbreakers. This can include those in authority breaking the law with impunity, knowing that there will be no consequences.

> Because of the increase of wickedness, the love of most will grow cold, but the one who stands firm to the end will be saved. (Matthew 24:12–13)

The word translated "wickedness" is the exact same word used of the man of lawlessness. It literally should be translated, "Because of the increase in lawlessness..." The idea that "the love of most will grow cold" specifically points toward believers. Non-believers may love friends and family, but this passage is speaking of the love of God. The love of believers growing cold reminds us of Revelation and the Laodiceans whose love was lukewarm. Love that is cold is worse than the lukewarm love of the Laodiceans. This is the reason that Jesus was pessimistic about the church at the time of His return.

And the Lord said, "Listen to what the unjust judge says. And will not God bring about justice for his chosen ones, who cry out to him day and night? Will he keep putting them off? I tell you, he will see that they get justice, and quickly. However, *when the Son of Man comes, will he find faith on the earth?*" (Luke 18:6–8, *emphasis added*)

THE ANTICHRIST

The third sign of the return of Christ is the revealing of the Antichrist. As we consider this, we should begin by recognizing that the term antichrist appears only in 1 John and 2 John. There are other references to a figure who attacks the church in other parts of Scripture (Daniel, 1 Thessalonians, etc.) who it appears is the antichrist, but only John uses that word. If we consider what John says there are a number of things we can recognize about the Antichrist.

Dear children, this is the last hour; and as you have heard that the antichrist is coming, even now many antichrists have come. This is how we know it is the last hour. They went out from us, but they did not really belong to us. For if they had belonged to us, they would have remained with us; but their going showed that none of them belonged to us. But you have an anointing from the Holy One, and all of you know the truth. I do not write to you because you do not know the truth, but because you do know it and because no lie comes from the truth. Who is the liar? It is whoever denies that Jesus is the Christ. Such a person is the antichrist—denying the Father and the Son. No one who denies the Son has the Father; whoever acknowledges the Son has the Father also. (1 John 2:18–23)

From this passage we see several things:

07: INTERPRETING REVELATION

- There are many antichrists
- There is someone John calls "the Antichrist" this person is distinguished from the many antichrists.
- The Antichrist *is coming* but the many antichrists *have come.*
- One attribute of an/the antichrist is that he/she went out from us, meaning they were part of the church and then denied the faith.
- Another is that he/she denies Jesus is the Christ.

We get additional insight from 2 John 1:7:

I say this because many deceivers, who do not acknowledge Jesus Christ as coming in the flesh, have gone out into the world. Any such person is the deceiver and the antichrist.

It appears from 2 John 1:7 that at least one thing the antichrists do is deny that Jesus has come in the flesh. This may have had particular application for Gnostics of John's time, but it has the potential to apply to future antichrist(s).

The first important insight we get from this is that the various people offered as possibly being "The Antichrist" are disqualified if they did not come out of the church. Figures proposed like Nero, Bill Gates, and whatever other secular figures are proposed are disqualified by John. That is devastating to views like Preterism.

The second insight is that there are many people throughout the ages who have come out of the church. Their denial of Christ makes them antichrists with a small "a." They are models of the ultimate Antichrist without actually being that person.

It also appears that Paul connects the coming of the Antichrist with rebellion.

Don't let anyone deceive you in any way, for *that day will not come until the rebellion occurs and the man of lawlessness is revealed,* the man doomed to destruction. (2 Thessalonians 2:3, *emphasis added*)

We should note that Paul speaks of "the rebellion" rather than a rebellion and the word used in the Greek is the word from which we get the word apostasy. This appears to me to refer to a rebellion in the church rather than in some political arena.

To recognize The Antichrist we need to know what kind of person we are expecting. In Revelation he is described as having two horns like a lamb and voice like a dragon.

> Then I saw a second beast, coming out of the earth. It had two horns like a lamb, but it spoke like a dragon. It exercised all the authority of the first beast on its behalf, and made the earth and its inhabitants worship the first beast, whose fatal wound had been healed. And *it performed great signs*, even causing fire to come down from heaven to the earth in full view of the people. (Revelation 13:11–13, *emphasis added*)

> The coming of the lawless one will be in accordance with how Satan works. He will use all sorts of *displays of power through signs and wonders* that serve the lie, and all the ways that wickedness deceives those who are perishing. They perish because they refused to love the truth and so be saved. For this reason, God sends them a powerful delusion so that they will believe the lie . . . (2 Thessalonians 2:9–11, *emphasis added*)

From these passages we see that one characteristic of the Antichrist is that he performs great signs. So one element in recognizing the Antichrist is that he displays power beyond human ability.

In Scripture, horns represent authority. So David speaks of horns as the power or authority of the wicked.

> To the arrogant I say, 'Boast no more,' and to the wicked, 'Do not lift up your *horns*.
> Do not lift your *horns* against heaven; do not speak so defiantly.'"

As for me, I will declare this forever; I will sing praise to the God of Jacob, who says, "I will cut off the *horns* of all the wicked, but the *horns* of the righteous will be lifted up." (Psalm 75:4f, 9f *emphasis added*)

In Revelation the image of horns like a lamb represents two sources of authority. Since the lamb represents Jesus in Revelation, those two sources of authority would be two portions of Christ's church.

In Revelation, the dragon represents Satan. One who speaks like a dragon would be someone who says things inspired by Satan. That leads us to expect that this antichrist figure may be a religious leader who leads two parts of Christ's church, yet says things that are satanic. He dazzles people by performing signs and wonders.

By understanding how these images connect to the rest of Scripture, we may be able to read Revelation and the other eschatological passages in Daniel, the Gospels, and in Paul's letters without having pre-existing ideas that block us from reading the biblical text objectively.

Below are a few rules that help the student of Revelation interpret the text.

INTERNAL CONSISTENCY

Images that appear elsewhere in Scripture, especially in apocalyptic texts, should be presumed to have a similar meaning to the same images that appear within Revelation. The term "apocalyptic" refers to writings, sometimes making extensive use of imagery, which describe the end of the world. The apocalyptic material in Revelation often stands on the foundation of apocalyptic images from the Old and New Testaments. That is not to say that John wrote with certain images in mind—he wrote down what he saw in his vision. But God communicated through the vision so that John was able to understand much of what he saw, based on God's use of images from the Old and New Testament Scriptures.

To give you an example, in Revelation there are three references to a figure wielding an iron scepter.

The one who conquers and who keeps my works until the end, to him *I will give authority over the nations*, and *he will rule them with a rod of iron*, as when earthen pots are broken in pieces, even as I myself have received authority from my Father. And I will give him the morning star. (Revelation 2:26–28 ESV, *emphasis added*)

She gave birth to a male child, *one who is to rule all the nations with a rod of iron*, but her child was caught up to God and to his throne, and the woman fled into the wilderness, where she has a place prepared by God, in which she is to be nourished for 1,260 days. (Revelation 12:5–6 ESV, *emphasis added*)

Then I saw heaven opened, and behold, a white horse! The one sitting on it is *called Faithful and True*, and in righteousness he judges and makes war. His eyes are like a flame of fire, and on his head are many diadems, and he has a name written that no one knows but himself. He is clothed in a robe dipped in blood, and *the name by which he is called is The Word of God*. And *the armies of heaven*, arrayed in fine linen, white and pure, *were following him* on white horses. From his mouth comes a sharp sword with which to strike down the nations, and *he will rule them with a rod of iron*. He will tread the winepress of the fury of the wrath of God the Almighty. On his robe and on his thigh *he has a name written, King of kings and Lord of lords*. (Revelation 19:11–16 ESV, *emphasis added*)

The image of the figure with the iron scepter comes from Psalm 2:7–9 (see also Hebrews 1:5):

I will tell of the decree:
The Lord said to me, "You are my Son;
today I have begotten you.
Ask of me, and I will make the nations your heritage,
and the ends of the earth your possession.

07: INTERPRETING REVELATION

You shall break them with a rod of iron
and dash them in pieces like a potter's vessel." (ESV)

We know this Psalm refers to Jesus, because Hebrews 1:5 tells us it does. But when we read Revelation 19:15, we can see that the figure described as ruling with a rod of iron is Jesus, the Son of God. Psalm 2, where the Lord addresses one He calls His Son, simply affirms what we see in Revelation 19.

PRIOR DEFINITION

If the meaning of an image is defined within apocalyptic material, the same image has the same meaning throughout the document. For example, the image of the seven lampstands in Revelation 1 is defined as seven churches. Therefore, when lampstands are used symbolically in Revelation 11:4, we can assume that these lampstands also refer to churches. It is this element of consistency that makes apocalyptic material understandable.

Scholarly documents or textbooks tend to define terms the first time they appear. In Revelation, images are sometimes defined after they have been used several times. Images that appear at the beginning of Revelation are sometimes not defined until near the end. In such cases, knowledge of the whole book is necessary to interpret symbols found at the beginning of the book. When John does not provide a definition, he assumes that an image in Revelation needs no definition. Either the image exists elsewhere in Scripture or its meaning can be understood from the context.

DO NOT PRESUME TO KNOW MORE THAN JESUS

Jesus clearly stated that he did not know the day or hour of his return.

But concerning that day and hour no one knows, not even the angels of heaven, nor the Son, but the Father only. (Matthew 24:36 ESV)

If He who was the perfect Son of God did not know, it is presumptive for someone else to suggest that he knows what Jesus did not. Jesus had several advantages that are not available to the modern biblical scholar:

- Jesus was unfallen and without sin, so He could understand the Scriptures as God's Word better than anyone else. He would not have the blind spots that fallen men have because of their sins.
- Jesus, as a prophet of God, was able to know things that others did not. If it had been God's intention to communicate the day and time of Christ's return, God would have given that information to Jesus. Jesus would have handled that information with wisdom and discretion superior to that of any modern man.
- Jesus' knowledge of the Old Testament and of those texts derived from His teaching would have to be superior to that of any interpreter today. Jesus would have known the information contained in those portions of the New Testament where He is quoted or where the Old Testament is quoted or referred to. There are few texts that could possibly have contained information that Jesus would not have known during His earthly ministry (such as those portions of Paul's writings, the other epistles, and Revelation that are not directly derived from the Old Testament or from Jesus' teaching). Those few texts do not appear to provide detailed chronological information that would allow anyone to determine the day or hour of Jesus' return.

REFERENCES TO TIME IN REVELATION

Most references to time in Revelation are symbolic and do not give an exact chronology of events. References to time can be considered symbolic when the length of time is a large number rounded to the nearest one thousand or when the period is indefinite (as in "time, times, and half a time"). These references also can be recognized as symbolic when they come from biblical passages outside Revelation where they are used symbolically (again, as in "time, times, and half a time"). They are symbolic when the same unit of time in different forms (such as 1,260 days and fortytwo months) is connected to symbolic references to time.

> The woman fled into the wilderness, where she has a place prepared by God, in which *she is to be nourished for 1,260 days*. (Revelation 12:6 ESV, *emphasis added*)

> But the woman was given the two wings of the great eagle so that she might fly from the serpent into the wilderness, to the place *where she is to be nourished for a time, and times, and half a time*. (Revelation 12:14 ESV, *emphasis added*)

How do we know that "times, times, and half a time" is symbolic? The handling of references to time in eschatological texts elsewhere in Scripture (like Daniel) is a clue to how they should be handled in Revelation.

Daniel uses the phrase "time, times, and half a time" in two of his visions. Where it appears, it refers to two different periods.

> After them another king will arise, different from the earlier ones; he will subdue three kings. He will speak against the Most High and oppress his holy people and try to change the set times and the laws. The holy people will be delivered into his hands for a *time, times and half a time*.
>
> "But the court will sit, and his power will be taken away and completely destroyed forever. Then the sovereignty, power and greatness of all the kingdoms under heaven will be handed over to the holy people of the Most High. His kingdom will be an everlasting kingdom, and all rulers will worship and obey him." (Daniel 7:24b–27, *emphasis added*)

In this passage, "time, times, and half a time" describes the period during which the saints are handed over to the man of lawlessness. He is destroyed and an everlasting kingdom is established.

> Then I, Daniel, looked, and there before me stood two others, one on this bank of the river and one on the opposite bank. One of them said to the man clothed in linen, who was above the waters of the river, "*How long will it be before these astonishing things are fulfilled?*"
>
> The man clothed in linen, who was above the waters of the river, lifted his right hand and his left hand toward heaven, and I heard him swear by him who lives forever, saying, "*It will be for a time, times and half a time.* When the power of the *holy people* has been finally broken, all these things will be completed." (Daniel 12:5–7, *emphasis added*)

One of the two other men asks how long (from the day of the vision) it will be before these things are fulfilled. The answer is not that at the end of human history it will be for time, times, and half a time. The period described begins in Daniel's time and comes to its completion when the power of the holy people is finally broken. This measure of time describes two different periods, but it ends at the same time.

In Revelation, the purpose of John's vision is not to tell when everything will happen. Jesus' promise that all these things will come soon provides sufficient warning that believers should be ready when the Lord returns. The important issue is not when things will happen, but what things will happen. This is why the references to time in Revelation are almost all symbolic. As symbols, they do not define specific dates and times, but they do describe a series of interconnected events. This approach allows the believer to see that God planned all events, and they are in His hands. This assurance will help the church, as it faces persecution, to endure patiently until the end.

07: INTERPRETING REVELATION

CONSIDER TO WHOM THE BOOK IS ADDRESSED

Passages that contain apocalyptic material were understood to some extent by the people to whom they were sent. New Testament passages were written for an audience that would directly benefit from those teachings. It is also relevant for modern Christians, and that is part of what makes Scripture unique.

Some have wanted to treat Revelation as though it was a letter addressed to the modern church. While some prophetic elements have not been fulfilled and will be fulfilled in the future, the book must belong primarily to the seven churches. John wrote Revelation for the seven churches, and it deals with particular situations they faced. As with the Corinthian letters and Paul's other letters, the modern reader is reading someone else's mail. It is to God's glory that "someone else's mail" is profitable to the church of the twentieth and twenty-first centuries for teaching, rebuking, correcting, and training in righteousness (2 Tim. 3:16).

We can distinguish passages within Revelation that pertain to the end of the world and the second coming from those that do not. Frequently, texts describing the culmination of human history directly refer to the judgment at the end of the world or to Christ's return. These texts typically include extreme language tied to a judgment theme, or a description of the coming of the Lord and the fear experienced by His enemies. Some texts also describe the ascension of the church into heaven or a song of celebration that the Lord is reigning. The faithful in the seven churches are connected to the end of the world by being promised things that those who endure until the end receive (e.g., to eat from the tree of life, or to sit with Jesus on His throne). We cannot assume that because a text is in Revelation it automatically has something to do with the end of the world.

OLD TESTAMENT FULFILLMENT

One difficulty in interpreting Old Testament passages that may pertain to the end of the world lies in knowing exactly which passages have been fulfilled and which await fulfillment. Old Testament prophecies that refer to God's judgment on Israel and other nations should be largely, if not entirely, fulfilled by now. This is particularly true when the nation prophesied against was later destroyed by a competing nation or empire. It is not always clear how a passage was fulfilled. But we can know that material has been fulfilled if it describes how God will judge particular nations that no longer exist. Some readers are comfortable proposing the reconstruction of ancient kingdoms. However, it seems that if that was what the text was describing, such a reconstruction would itself require a separate prophecy.

Some Old Testament texts clearly refer to the final judgment, God descending with His holy ones, or the ultimate purification and vindication of Israel. Some of these passages include a description of how local nations which no longer exist acted against the people of God. However, the primary focus of those passages is God's judgment of the nations of the world, the purification of Israel, and the establishment of an idealized world blessed by God. These texts do have eschatological relevance and should be used with New Testament eschatological passages to build a fully developed theology of the end of the world. Typically, images or teachings from relevant Old Testament texts are used in Revelation.

Additionally, you should never assume dual fulfillment unless Scripture describes a passage as having been fulfilled twice. In Matthew 2:14–15 we see dual fulfillment, where the prophecy quoted from Hosea refers to both Israel and Jesus.

> So he got up, took the child and his mother during the night and left for Egypt, where he stayed until the death of Herod. And so was fulfilled what the Lord had said through the prophet: "Out of Egypt I called my son."

We would never have gotten that interpretation from reading Hosea 11:1 alone, but because Scripture describes the events in Matthew as a second fulfillment, we know that it is. Interestingly, a significant number of end times views depend on second fulfillment in order for their position to survive.

07: INTERPRETING REVELATION

CONSIDER THE CONTEXT OF THE PASSAGE

Almost any meaning can be derived from reading a short section of Scripture in isolation. For any interpretation to be valid, it has to be consistent with the meaning of the surrounding passages. This is true even of Revelation. John's vision contains a number of revelatory units (e.g., seven seals, seven trumpets, and seven bowls). Some interpreters have strung together a series of passages to prove a particular eschatological view. The verses tied together and in isolation from other texts can be convincing. However, a comparison of the meaning of those passages with their context discredits the interpretation.

EXTREME LANGUAGE

"Extreme language" is a term that describes a devastating series of signs in the heavens and on earth. These events can include earthquakes, thunder and lightning, hailstorms, and dramatic changes in the sun, moon, and stars. The question is, are the descriptions of these extreme events intended to be taken literally?

The interpretation of extreme language in the New Testament should be consistent with its use throughout the Old Testament where it refers to historical events. In Revelation 6:12–14 the sun is darkened, the moon is turned blood red, and the stars fall to the earth. Similar language appears in Matthew 24:29, and Mark 13:24–25, and there is a reference to it in Luke 21:25. The language in these New Testament passages is similar to that used to describe the destruction prophesied in Isaiah 13:9–13, concerning the Lord's overthrow of Babylon.

> The stars of heaven and their constellations
> will not show their light.
> The rising sun will be darkened
> and the moon will not give its light. (Isaiah 13:10)

There is no indication in historical records that the signs in the heavens described in Isaiah 13 literally occurred immediately prior to Babylon's destruction. Likewise, extreme language is used in Isaiah 34 to describe God's destruction of all the nations, but especially of Edom.

> Edom's streams will be turned into pitch,
> her dust into burning sulfur;
> her land will become burning pitch!
> It will not be quenched night and day;
> its smoke will rise forever.
> From generation to generation it will lie desolate;
> no one will ever pass through it again. (Isaiah 34:9–10)

Edom was judged and destroyed, but the land has not been turned into burning pitch. Ezekiel 32:7–8 uses similar language of God's judgment on Egypt.

> When I snuff you out, I will cover the heavens
> and darken their stars;
> I will cover the sun with a cloud,
> and the moon will not give its light.
> All the shining lights in the heavens
> I will darken over you;
> I will bring darkness over your land,
> declares the Sovereign Lord. (Ezekiel 32:7–8)

Egypt has been judged and destroyed, but the events in the heavens that were described did not literally occur. The judgments pronounced in all these passages occurred without the literal darkening of the heavens or the literal burning of the land. From this it can be concluded that the language was not intended to be taken literally. Its purpose is to describe the extreme chaos that results from the destruction of a nation or world power. Regarding the Babylonians God says:

> See I will stir up against them the Medes, who do not care for silver and have no delight in gold. (Isaiah 13:17)

History tells us that the Medes and Persians conquered the Babylonians. The context of Ezekiel's prophecy also supports its fulfillment at the time it was made. Ezekiel prophesied after Babylon captured Jerusalem. Speaking to Egypt, which failed to help Israel against Babylon, he says:

> For this is what the Sovereign Lord says:
> "The sword of the king of Babylon
> will come against you." (Ezekiel 32:11)

History tells us that Babylon conquered Egypt after capturing Jerusalem. The judgment of these nations has already come just as the prophecy stated. Therefore, it is reasonable to assert that the literal fulfillment of the extreme language in the prophecy was not intended.

The purpose of extreme language is to communicate the devastating nature of God's judgment. God's judgment on nations has been so severe that it would seem to those judged as though the sun was darkened and the stars were falling from the sky. This does not mean that the Old Testament images cannot literally come true at the end of human history. It is prophesied in several places in the Old Testament, and in Revelation, that there will be a great earthquake at the very end (Ezek. 38:19; Zech. 14:3–5; Rev. 6:12; 11:13,19; 16:18). There is every reason to believe that there will be an earthquake at the end of history. The possible literal fulfillment of some extreme language at the end of human history does not diminish its significance as language that throughout Scripture symbolizes judgment by the Lord.

Revelation is one of the most difficult books in the Bible to interpret, but when we're willing to remove our theological filters and read it in the context of the rest of Scripture, we're likely to find things in Revelation that we've missed.

08

HARMONIZING PASSAGES

The Gospels contain what are called parallel passages. These are accounts in Matthew, Mark, and Luke (the Synoptic Gospels) and sometimes John that appear to describe the same events in Jesus' life. Many people come to the parallel passages and automatically assume that these passages are describing the same events. Sometimes they are, but sometimes they are not. There are often variations in the parallel passages that seem hard to reconcile.

One of the approaches used to deal with apparent discrepancies in the Gospels is called harmonization. In harmonization we look at two passages in different Gospels that appear to describe the same event and consider how they are the same and how the differences between them can be reconciled.

Harmonizing discrepancies must not be done "at all costs" to avoid any sense that there is a problem in the text. Some interpreters have been intellectually dishonest in using harmonization, and they produce results that are clearly not consistent with the biblical text.

There are a number of ways that passages can be harmonized.

COMPARISON OF THE DETAILS

Sometimes the details in a passage signify that parallel passages may not actually be two records of the same events. Let's consider Matthew 20:29-34, Mark 10:46-52, and Luke 18:35-43, which are parallel passages that contain obvious differences.

> And as they went out of Jericho, a great crowd followed him. And behold, there were two blind men sitting by the roadside, and when they heard that Jesus was passing by, they cried out, "Lord, have mercy on us, Son of David!" The crowd rebuked them, telling them to be silent, but they cried out all the more, "Lord, have mercy on us, Son of David!" And stopping, Jesus called them and said, "What do you want me to do for you?" They said to him, "Lord, let our eyes be opened." And Jesus in pity touched their eyes, and immediately they recovered their sight and followed him. (Matthew 20:29–34 ESV)

> And they came to Jericho. And as he was leaving Jericho with his disciples and a great crowd, Bartimaeus, a blind beggar, the son of Timaeus, was sitting by the roadside. And when he heard that it was Jesus of Nazareth, he began to cry out and say, "Jesus, Son of David, have mercy on me!" And many rebuked him, telling him to be silent. But he cried out all the more, "Son of David, have mercy on me!" And Jesus stopped and said, "Call him." And they called the blind man, saying to him, "Take heart. Get up; he is calling you." And throwing off his cloak, he sprang up and came to Jesus. And Jesus said to him, "What do you want me to do for you?" And the blind man said to him, "Rabbi, let me recover my sight." And Jesus said to him, "Go your way; your faith has made you well." And immediately he recovered his sight and followed him on the way. (Mark 10:46–52 ESV)

> As he drew near to Jericho, a blind man was sitting by the roadside begging. And hearing a crowd going by, he inquired what this meant. They told him, "Jesus of Nazareth is passing by." And he cried out, "Jesus, Son of David, have mercy on me!" And those who were in front rebuked him, telling him to be silent. But he cried out all the more, "Son of David, have mercy on me!" And Jesus stopped and commanded him to be brought to him. And when he came near, he asked him,

08: HARMONIZING PASSAGES

"What do you want me to do for you?" He said, "Lord, let me recover my sight." And Jesus said to him, "Recover your sight; your faith has made you well." And immediately he recovered his sight and followed him, glorifying God. And all the people, when they saw it, gave praise to God. (Luke 18:35–43 ESV)

These passages are parallel, but they don't seem to agree. There are two blind men in the Matthew passage, but one in the other texts. In Matthew and Mark, Jesus is leaving Jericho, but in Luke He is approaching Jericho.

HOW SHOULD WE MAKE SENSE OF THE APPARENT DISCREPANCIES IN THESE PASSAGES?

Matthew and Mark may be describing the same event: Peter knew Bartimaeus, presumably because Bartimaeus became a follower of Jesus, and so in Peter's account (the Gospel of Mark), he focuses on the man he knew by name. Matthew tells us there were two blind men. He could be describing a different event, or there could have been another blind man with Bartimaeus. In contrast, Luke is describing a completely different event. In Matthew and Mark, Jesus meets the blind men as He is leaving the city. In Luke, Jesus meets the blind man as He approaches Jericho. We must be careful not to try to force parallel passages to be identical when they are in the same place in the Gospels but are not describing the same events.

When we harmonize a passage, we are not merely looking at differences. One of the objectives of harmonization is to understand how God has provided a richness to the account. We want to see how God uses what some might call discrepancies to give us more information in the different Gospels.

HARMONIZING PETER'S DENIAL

Let's look at an event recorded in all the Gospels that has caused many people difficulty as they tried to harmonize the accounts. One conservative author even attempted to harmonize these passages by claiming that Peter denied the Lord six times! These texts show us how variations can come from different perspectives of an event. They also give us an example of how more detail in one truly parallel passage can add to what we know.

> Now Peter was sitting out in the courtyard, and *a servant girl* came to him. "You also were with Jesus of Galilee," she said.
> But *he denied it before them all.* "I don't know what you're talking about," he said.
> Then he went out to the gateway, where *another servant girl* saw him and *said to the people there*, "This fellow was with Jesus of Nazareth." He denied it again, with an oath: "I don't know the man!"
> After a little while, *those standing there* went up to Peter and said, "Surely you are one of them; *your accent gives you away*."
> Then he began to call down curses, and he swore to them, "I don't know the man!" *Immediately a rooster crowed.* Then Peter remembered the word Jesus had spoken: "Before the rooster crows, you will disown me three times." And he went outside and wept bitterly. (Matthew 26:69–75, *emphasis added*)

> While Peter was below in the courtyard, *one of the servant girls* of the high priest came by. When she saw Peter warming himself, she looked closely at him.
> "You also were with that Nazarene, Jesus," she said.
> But *he denied it.* "I don't know or understand what you're talking about," he said, and went out into the entryway. When *the servant girl* saw him there, she *said again to those standing around*, "This fellow is one of them." Again he denied it.
> After a little while, *those standing near* said to Peter, "Surely you are one of them, for *you are a Galilean*."
> He began to call down curses, and he swore to them, "I don't know this man you're talking about."
> *Immediately the rooster crowed the second time.* Then Peter remembered the word Jesus had spoken to him: "Before the rooster crows twice you will disown me three times." And he broke down and wept.

(Mark 14:66-72, *emphasis added*)

Then seizing him, they led him away and took him into the house of the high priest. Peter followed at a distance. And when some there had kindled a fire in the middle of the courtyard and had sat down together, Peter sat down with them. *A servant girl* saw him seated there in the firelight. She looked closely at him and said, *"This man was with him."*
 But *he denied it.* "Woman, I don't know him," he said. A little later *someone else* saw him and said, "You also are one of them."
 "Man, I am not!" Peter replied.
 About an hour later *another asserted*, "Certainly this fellow was with him, for *he is a Galilean."*
 Peter replied, "Man, I don't know what you're talking about!" *Just as he was speaking, the rooster crowed. The Lord turned and looked straight at Peter.* Then Peter remembered the word the Lord had spoken to him: "Before the rooster crows today, you will disown me three times." And he went outside and wept bitterly. (Luke 22:54-62, emphasis added)

The other disciple, who was known to the high priest, came back, spoke to the *servant girl* on duty there and brought Peter in. "You aren't one of this man's disciples too, are you?" she asked Peter.
 He replied, "I am not."
 It was cold, and the servants and officials stood around a fire they had made to keep warm. Peter also was standing with them, warming himself...
 Meanwhile, Simon Peter was still standing there warming himself. So *they asked him*, "You aren't one of his disciples too, are you?"
 He denied it, saying, "I am not."
 One of the high priest's servants, a relative of the man whose ear Peter had cut off, challenged him, "Didn't I see you with him in the garden?" Again Peter denied it, and *at that moment a rooster began to crow.* (John 18:16b-18, 25-27, *emphasis added*)

There are four points in each of the Gospels that we will need to reconcile with each other. There are three confrontations that result in Peter denying the Lord, and at the conclusion the cock crows.

PETER'S FIRST DENIAL

Peter first denies Jesus to a servant or slave girl. John says she asked Peter if he was a disciple too, suggesting that she knew John was one of Jesus' disciples. In Mark, she says Peter was with Jesus. In Luke, she speaks to the crowd, and in Matthew, Peter denies Jesus before "them all." How do we harmonize these differences?

In all four Gospels, a servant girl asked Peter if he was a follower of Jesus. John provides the most details, saying she asked as John brought Peter into the area where the trial was going on. We see here, and later in all the passages, that there were others in the courtyard. Peter's denial did not convince the servant girl, because she spoke to others saying this man was with them. That is why Matthew mentions that Peter denied it before them all.

We might want to think that the denials were simple. A question was asked and answered with no complications. But in a crowded area, a question that piques the interest of many who are present will draw others into the conversation. Peter answered the question, not just to the girl but in front of the onlookers. Peter did not like where this was going, so Mark tells us that Peter walked away, afraid she would persist.

And when she saw him again later, she did persist (Mark 14:68–69).

PETER'S SECOND DENIAL

This denial is more challenging to harmonize. John shows a crowd addressing Peter; Matthew introduces another servant girl, different from the first who accused him. Mark features a persistent maid, the same as the one who first asked, and Luke shows Peter responding to a man. How do we harmonize these passages?

In both Matthew and Mark, the servant girl addresses those who were there, not Peter. It does not require any great imagination to believe that more than one woman may have asserted Peter's involvement with Jesus to the crowd. Since at least two women are speaking to the crowd, saying that Peter is one of Jesus' followers, we would expect the crowd to get involved. As often happens in crowds, one person takes the lead and, as a representative of them all, asks Peter if the allegations were true.

We could expect that leader to be a man, since this occurred in a male-dominated society. It seems reasonable, given the way crowd dynamics usually work, to assume that the crowd would shout out questions. Luke could be describing the question addressed by a leader, while John describes questions asked by both the leader and by others in the crowd.

PETER'S THIRD DENIAL

This denial has a similar diversity in the questions being asked of Peter.

Luke shows another man insisting that Peter was a follower of Jesus; John features a relative of the man whose ear Peter cut off insisting. Matthew and Mark show the bystanders again addressing Peter, saying that Peter's accent gives him away. Again, each Gospel writer is able to accurately describe the story from a different point of view.

It is not difficult to reconstruct that there was a particular man to whom Peter responded. This man could have been, but did not necessarily have to be, a relative of the servant of the high priest whose ear Peter cut off. The insistent man spoke to the bystanders, while the relative—whether he was someone different or not—spoke to Peter directly. In both the second and third denials Peter seems to be dealing with groups of people, which blurs the distinction of this person or that person asking a particular question. Several people may have said something, but the Gospel writers are under no obligation to report everything that was said in such a confused setting. Each one accurately reports the story as described by the eyewitnesses who were their sources.

DIFFERENCES IN THE NUMBER OF TIMES THE COCK CROWED

Only Mark reports that the cock crowed twice. As we look at variances in the numbers, we should be careful not to draw lines any finer than those drawn by the text. Mark says the cock crowed twice, but none of the other texts say that the cock crowed once and only once.

It appears as though Peter denied the Lord and then the cock crowed. If we did not have Mark, we could reasonably assume that the denial took place before the first crowing of the cock. But our interpretive principle here is that greater detail in one text should be applied to other truly parallel passages.

In most situations we need to ensure that the same event is being described, because sometimes parallel passages are not truly parallel. We must also be sure the accounts depict events occurring at the same time. If we see different details in the description of what is going on, we might be seeing something that happened earlier on the same day.

But in this case, Mark is providing additional details about the circumstances surrounding Peter's denial. Mark, who is writing Peter's Gospel, quotes Jesus as saying that before the cock crowed twice, Peter would deny him three times. Those who did not hear Jesus' words reported what they heard from Peter after the fact. Everyone knew the big picture. Peter denied the Lord three times before the cock crowed. Peter, being human, gave a summary of the events to his friends, without going into minute details. It was, after all, an embarrassing event in Peter's life. But when Mark recorded Peter's Gospel, Peter may have provided the additional detail that Jesus had told him that the denial would precede the cock crowing twice.

Luke provides an additional detail by recording that, as Peter was speaking, a cock crowed and Jesus turned and looked straight at Peter. At that point Peter remembered that Jesus had said, "Before the rooster crows today, you will disown me three times."

HARMONIZING MATTHEW AND LUKE IN LIGHT OF DANIEL

Sometimes harmonizing requires a Scripture interprets Scripture approach, because outside passages explain the significance of the texts we are harmonizing. For example, let's look at how two passages in the New Testament can be harmonized with the help of Daniel 10–12.

"So when you see standing in the holy place 'the *abomination that causes desolation*,' spoken of through the prophet *Daniel*—let the reader understand—then let those who are in Judea flee to the mountains. *Let no one on the housetop go down to take anything out of the house. Let no one in the field go back to get their cloak.* How dreadful it will be in those days for pregnant women and nursing mothers! *Pray that your flight will not take place in winter or on the Sabbath.* For then there will be great distress, unequaled from the beginning of the world until now—and never to be equaled again.

"If those days had not been cut short, no one would survive, but for the sake of the elect those days will be shortened. At that time if anyone says to you, 'Look, here is the Messiah!' or, 'There he is!' do not believe it. For false messiahs and false prophets will appear and perform great signs and wonders to deceive, if possible, even the elect. See, I have told you ahead of time.

"So if anyone tells you, 'There he is, out in the wilderness,' do not go out; or, 'Here he is, in the inner rooms,' do not believe it. *For as lightning that comes from the east is visible even in the west, so will be the coming of the Son of Man.* Wherever there is a carcass, there the *vultures will gather.* (Matthew 24:15–28, *emphasis added*)

"*But before all this*, they will seize you and persecute you. They will hand you over to synagogues and put you in prison, and you will be brought before kings and governors, and all on account of my name. And so you will bear testimony to me. But make up your mind not to worry beforehand how you will defend yourselves. For I will give you words and wisdom that none of your adversaries will be able to resist or contradict. You will be betrayed even by parents, brothers and sisters, relatives and friends, and they will put some of you to death. Everyone will hate you because of me. But not a hair of your head will perish. Stand firm, and you will win life.

"When you see *Jerusalem being surrounded by armies*, you will know that *its desolation* is near. Then let those who are in Judea flee to the mountains, let those in the city get out, and let those in the country not enter the city. For this is the time of punishment in fulfillment of all that has been written. How dreadful it will be in those days for pregnant women and nursing mothers! There will be great distress in the land and *wrath against this people.* They will fall by the sword and *will be taken as prisoners to all the nations.* Jerusalem will be trampled on by the Gentiles until the *times of the Gentiles* are fulfilled. (Luke 21:12–24, *emphasis added*)

For *the Son of Man in his day will be like the lightning, which flashes and lights up the sky from one end to the other.* But first he must suffer many things and be rejected by this generation. "Just as it was in the days of Noah, so also will it be in the days of the Son of Man. People were eating, drinking, marrying and being given in marriage up to the day Noah entered the ark. Then the flood came and destroyed them all.

"It was the same in the days of Lot. People were eating and drinking, buying and selling, planting and building. But the day Lot left Sodom, fire and sulfur rained down from heaven and destroyed them all.

"It will be just like this on the day the Son of Man is revealed. On that day *no one who is on the housetop, with possessions inside, should go down to get them. Likewise, no one in the field should go back for anything.* Remember Lot's wife! Whoever tries to keep their life will lose it, and whoever loses their life will preserve it. I tell you, on that night two people will be in one bed; one will be taken and the other left. Two women will be grinding grain together; one will be taken and the other left."

"Where, Lord?" they asked.

He replied, "Where there is a dead body, there the *vultures will gather.*" (Luke 17:24–37, *emphasis added*)

I encourage you to read Daniel 10–12 alongside these passages and notice, as we compare them, that the abomination that causes desolation mentioned in Matthew 24:15 must be a reference to Daniel 9:27 and the vision in Daniel 10-12. Additionally, Jesus' reference to the time of distress comes from Daniel 12:1. Whatever it is, per Daniel, some abomination is "set up" at the temple.

Most people view Matthew 24 and Luke 21 as parallel passages. But if we compare Matthew 24:15-28 with Luke 21:12-24, and consider how they differ, it may give us pause. If we come to the Luke text expecting it to be the same as the Matthew passage, we feel like we are affirmed when we compare Matthew 24:1-14 and Luke 21:5-11. Both passages begin by speaking of war, famines, and earthquakes. Later, both passages speak of pregnant women and nursing mothers. As we dig deeper, however, the language in the two passages points to different events.

TWO DIFFERENT DIRECTIONS

In Matthew 24, the disciples ask for a sign of Jesus' coming and of the end of the age. In Luke 21, the disciples ask when the stones of the temple will be thrown down and ask what will be the sign that it is about to take place. The early verses of both passages contain end times language. But toward the middle, in the portions provided above, the passages go in completely different directions. Matthew points to the setting up of the abomination that causes desolation spoken of in Daniel, while Luke speaks of the desolation of Jerusalem. It appears that Matthew, in verses 15-28, is talking about the end of human history, while Luke, in verses 12-24, is talking about the destruction of Jerusalem in 70 AD.

In Matthew 24, Jesus describes a need to flee that is so urgent that those who are on the roofs of their houses should flee down the outside staircase and not even go into their houses to try to save anything. In Luke 21, in contrast, Jesus urges his hearers to get out of the city when they see Jerusalem surrounded by armies. The level of urgency in Luke is far less than that described in Matthew. This is because Luke is describing the need to flee in the period leading up to 70 AD. In 68 AD, Nero died and the Roman armies left Israel for more than a year. So there was no urgency to leave Jerusalem in the period from 68 AD to 70 AD. People could pack bags, hire a cart, throw parties to say goodbye to family and friends, and still have plenty of time to get out of Jerusalem. Interestingly, Luke 17, which speaks of "the day the Son of Man is revealed," does speak of the need to flee and attaches an urgency similar to that found in Matthew.

Matthew encourages his readers to pray that their flight will not take place in winter (a season) or on the Sabbath (a day). This is because of the previously mentioned urgency. Luke makes no mention of this because the Romans are away for more than a year, so there would be no need to flee in winter or on a Sabbath.

Matthew also mentions that this time of distress is unequaled from the beginning of the world until now. In saying this, Matthew adds an interpretive element to Daniel 12:1:

> At that time Michael, the great prince who protects your people, will arise. There will be a time of distress such as has not happened from the beginning of nations until then. But at that time your people—everyone whose name is found written in the book—will be delivered. (Daniel 12:1)

The natural sense of this passage is that this will be a severe time of distress. Some interpreters minimize the distress and suggest that Daniel 12:1 refers to the 70 AD destruction of Jerusalem. That destruction was bad for those living there. But it was probably not even the worst destruction that Jerusalem had ever experienced. Matthew interprets the Daniel 12:1 passage, describing it as the worst distress ever in the history of the world.

It should be noted that Matthew's description of the signs of Jesus' coming and the end of the age do not in any way fit the events of 70 AD. The description of the time of distress doesn't fit 70 AD. Jesus' command to pray that this time of distress does not happen in winter or on the Sabbath in no way fits the siege of Jerusalem by the Romans in 70 AD. This is a significant problem for those holding the view called preterism.

Luke's great distress is "in this land" and the wrath is "against *this people*" (Luke 21:23). Because Luke is speaking of 70 AD, his distress is local and is directed against Israel. Luke is clearly including material not contained in Matthew. He is recording Jesus' warning about the 70 AD destruction of Jerusalem. He begins the section that starts in verse 12 with "But before all this," pointing to events that precede the events he has described in verses 8-11. In verse 24, he concludes this section with a reference to the Jews being carried off to all nations and Jerusalem being trampled by the Gentiles until the times of the Gentiles are fulfilled. The times of the Gentiles are also discussed in Romans 11 (see especially verses 25-29) and in Revelation 11:2, where the Gentiles trample Jerusalem for forty-two months. In verse 25, Luke returns to his previous theme—the great signs in heaven (Luke 21:11)—by discussing the signs in the sun, moon, and stars.

Matthew says that where there is a carcass, there the vultures will gather. Luke includes a similar statement in Luke 17. This image applies to the end of the world and so is not included in Luke 21. Interestingly, Daniel 12:7 speaks of the power of the holy people being broken in the context of the resurrection of the dead and the end of the world. This same concept has already been mentioned earlier in Daniel 7:25-27 and Daniel 8:23-25.

THE ABOMINATION THAT CAUSES DESOLATION

In Daniel 11:21-45, Daniel describes the king who sets up the abomination that causes desolation. This king of the north is a contemptible person not given the honor of royalty. He does a number of evil things and is successful until "the time of wrath" (v. 36) is completed. At "the time of the end" (v. 40), he invades the Beautiful Land (Israel) and pitches his tents at the beautiful holy mountain. He then comes to his end (v. 45). In the very next verse Daniel provides the context for what follows. He begins 12:1 by saying "At that time," meaning at the same time that the king of the north has come to his end, Michael will arise and there will begin a "time of distress such as has not happened from the beginning of nations until then." But "at that time," your people will be delivered (v. 2) by the resurrection of the dead.

The context of the abomination that causes desolation in Daniel 11 and 12 is the end of the world (as seen in the reference to the resurrection of the dead). Therefore, we should expect that, in Matthew, when Jesus refers to the abomination that causes desolation, he is talking about the end of human history. Further, Jesus' reference to the time of distress, which appears in the verse preceding the resurrection of the dead in Daniel 12, clarifies that indeed He is speaking of the end of the world and the final resurrection.

> *At that time* Michael, the great prince who protects your people, will arise. There will be a *time of distress* such as has not happened from the beginning of nations until then. But *at that time* your people—everyone whose name is found written in the book—will be delivered. *Multitudes who sleep in the dust of the earth will awake: some to everlasting life, others to shame and everlasting contempt.* Those who are wise will shine like the brightness of the heavens, and those who lead many to righteousness, like the stars for ever and ever. But you, Daniel, roll up and seal the words of the scroll *until the time of the end.* Many will go here and there to increase knowledge. (Daniel 12:1-4, emphasis added)

> From the time that the daily sacrifice is abolished and the *abomination that causes desolation* is set up, there will be 1,290 days. Blessed is the one who waits for and reaches the end of the 1,335 days. (Daniel 12:11-12, *emphasis added*)

Though harmonizing passages can be difficult—especially if those passages seem to contain discrepancies—it is worth the effort to do this well. Laying passages like these alongside one another and looking for contrasts as well as similarities can add greatly to our understanding of Scripture.

09

TRANSLATIONS AND OTHER STUDY TOOLS

We have a variety of English translations of the Bible available to us that can help us as we study the Scriptures. But not all of them are equally helpful. Clearly the most important thing in a translation is that it conveys to the reader the idea being communicated by the inspired writer. One school of thought argues that all a translation must do to be successful is accurately translate the words from the Greek or Hebrew biblical text. But is that really true?

Suppose you were reading a contemporary novel that was to be translated into another language, where two characters are in dialogue about some third person who has offered an explanation justifying why he did something wrong. The lead character turns to his friend and says, "That dog won't hunt." If you translate it precisely and literally into another language, particularly if the culture of those reading the translation is largely urban, or if dogs are viewed as nuisances or food, the readers will have no idea why the character is now talking about dogs.

We see the same thing in the Bible. In the wedding at Cana Jesus' mother suggests that he do something about the wine running out. Jesus responds literally, "What to me and to you woman?" The New American Standard Bible tried to maintain the literal sense.

On the third day there was a wedding in Cana of Galilee, and the mother of Jesus was there; and both Jesus and His disciples were invited to the wedding. When the wine ran out, the mother of Jesus said to Him, "They have no wine." And Jesus said to her, *"What business do you have with Me*, woman? My hour has not yet come." (John 2:1-4 NASB, *emphasis added*)

If you are like me, your response might be, "Jesus, is that any way to talk to your mother?" The problem is that the phrase, "What to me and to you" is an idiomatic phrase that is better captured in the English Standard Version.

On the third day there was a wedding at Cana in Galilee, and the mother of Jesus was there. Jesus also was invited to the wedding with his disciples. When the wine ran out, the mother of Jesus said to him, "They have no wine." And Jesus said to her, "Woman, *what does this have to do with me*? My hour has not yet come." (John 2:1-4 ESV, *emphasis added*)

On the opposite side of the spectrum are translations that take a larger portion of the text and rephrase the language in an effort to provide greater clarity and better literary flow of the text. The problem with this approach is that it inevitably includes the interpretation along with the translation. Sometimes these paraphrases get the interpretation right, but sometimes they get the interpretation wrong. In either case, it can be difficult to recognize what interpretive decisions have been made because the text seems to be clear.

The best translations have certain things in common.

- The biblical text presented reflects modern textual criticism. The text critical work will not be perfect, and each translation will not agree with each other in every detail, but they will be largely the same.
- The translators are literal in their translations but take into account non-literal language and accurately convey what the writer intended to say.

- The writing style is readable and designed to make it easier for the reader to memorize the text.
- The translation does not add words that are not in the Greek or Hebrew text, to accommodate modern cultural ideologies. While today we use more inclusive language, when Paul, writing in a male dominated society uses the term brothers, we should not correct that to brothers and sisters. That "correction" is the job of the modern interpreter (pastor, commentator, or bible student).

INTERLINEAR BIBLES

For many of the reasons provided above, an interlinear Bible, where the Greek text has an English translation of the Greek words below it, is generally not very helpful. We already saw the concern about the NASB, which translated the words literally but did not take into account the idiomatic phrasing. The same concern applies when the Greek text uses more complex grammatical structure. Of course, if you are studying ancient Greek and learning the forms and grammar, an interlinear Bible can help if you simply need assistance with vocabulary.

STUDY BIBLES

With the advent of so many versions of study Bibles, I would guess that most people own at least one study Bible. The study tools in those Bibles can be helpful. However, using a study Bible also presents a number of concerns.

- The study aids may not have enough space to present all the facts about controversial issues, such as the date a book was written. The book of Galatians was written somewhere between the late 40s AD to the late 50s AD. Likewise, the date the book of Revelation was written is controversial, and the range of possible dates is immense. Some have dated Revelation as early as 48 AD, while others propose that the book was written during the reign of Nero (54–68 AD). Still others hold that Revelation was written in 95 AD. A complete dis-

cussion of the various options and their merits would be difficult to include in a study Bible. Yet knowing the date the book was written can have a profound effect on how we interpret the book.
- The theology of the person writing the study guide will impact the content of the material. Their training, personal biases, and greater or lesser knowledge will appear in the study guide. In some cases, it can be difficult to distinguish opinion from fact.
- It is tempting to assume that the material is trustworthy simply because it is included in the study guide. It can be hard to separate the human element from the divinely inspired text of Scripture. We must remember that only portions of the study Bible are inspired, and those portions are the actual biblical text.

Additionally, the study guide can play into some of our worst traits.

We can become lazy and simply use the work already done in place of the hard work we are called to do in our study of God's Word. When we feel like we already have the answers available to us, we may fail to ask good questions or pay attention to details. For these reasons, I do not recommend using a study Bible.

As we put the strategies covered in this book to use, a trustworthy Bible translation can help us see the details in Scripture clearly and make connections within the text. A good translation, by leaving the interpretation to us, allows us to wrestle with difficult questions and parts of the text that are surprising. The closer a translation takes us to the actual words and meaning of the inspired writers, the greater the impact God's Word will have on our hearts.

CONCLUSION

Throughout this book, I have aimed not to criticize or to stoke controversy—or to suggest that I know something others don't—but to help us learn to recognize our own blind spots and to see the Bible clearly. Through the examples I've included in this book, I hope to show us that we do not see. Hopefully, that realization will motivate all of us to remove the filters that

09: TRANSLATIONS AND OTHER STUDY TOOLS

prevent us from seeing what is in the biblical text.

I just have to mention one more time how important the Bible is. Through the words of Scripture, God speaks to us in an active dialogue. We read a passage, and God uses our thoughts and life circumstances to help influence what we get out of it at that time. We respond to God's Word based on what we see, what we understand, and what seems best to us. A year later, we may read the same passage, and God may speak to us in a different way, through those same words, because the words haven't changed—but we have. We respond differently because God has put us in a different place. The ways our perception of Scripture changes affects our prayers and our actions toward God and others.

When we use the CLAP method, we are better equipped to hear God speak through His Word in the different seasons of our life. When we read each passage in Context, we gain a more complete understanding of the text. When we Look for what surprises us in God's Word, we approach the Bible expectantly. When we Ask difficult questions, we show integrity. And when we Pay attention to details, we value Scripture. All of these draw us closer to God, who communicates with us through His Word until we reach heaven.

Years ago, I spoke with a theologian who had written books and who was actively involved in Christian ministry. We spoke about a recent book that included some things that were challenging to certain traditional theological positions. He told me that he had been immersed in his theology for so long that he really couldn't look at the material in the book objectively or adjust his views. I hope you have not arrived at that place in your mind.

For seminary students, you have such an opportunity to read and study the Bible and theology. I would encourage you to take a balanced approach and seek out experienced pastors and teachers to talk to about the practical implications of living out the gospel. As you do your studies, I hope you are more involved in examining the Scriptures than in uncritically learning systems and rules in theology.

For pastors, what a joy it will be if you pay attention to details in the Bible that help you better understand how God works in the world. That attention can assist you as you take what you see in the text and talk about how we are to live that out in our homes, in our culture, and in the church at large. This would be such a benefit to those in your care who need to know not just what the Bible passages mean, but also what to do as a result. After all, the Scriptures help us in our joys and in our struggles. As Psalm 145 says,

> The Lord is trustworthy in all He promises
> and faithful in all He does.
> The Lord upholds all who fall
> and lifts up all who are bowed down. (vv. 13b–14)

To seminary professors and teachers, I understand the struggle. But can you allow the Scriptures to speak more loudly than what you already know? I hope you are humble enough to know your theology is not perfect, because none of us have perfect theology. Perhaps we can read more Scripture and fewer theology textbooks that repeat what we already believe.

Finally, I imagine this book will be read more by laypeople than by any other group. My hope is that you will start to see the things you haven't seen. I hope you will apply CLAP and, by doing so, will discover a renewed thrill in reading and studying the Scriptures. There is an excitement to finding new insights and seeing things we have never seen before.

> A voice says, "Cry out."
> And I said, "What shall I cry?"
> "All people are like grass,
> and all their faithfulness is like the flowers of the field.
> The grass withers and the flowers fall,
> because the breath of the Lord blows on them.
> Surely the people are grass.
> The grass withers and the flowers fall,
> *but the word of our God endures forever.*" (Isaiah 40:6–8, *emphasis added*)

I wish you joy as you read the Bible with new eyes. Amen.

MORE BOOKS FOR NEW EYES

THE END: A READER'S GUIDE TO REVELATION
"Anyone interested in the careful study of the Book of Revelation will find Alan Bauer's book both a helpful guide and a stimulating interpretation.... Read this book slowly, carefully, and you will find a rich banquet of insight and understanding."—T. M. Moore, a fellow of the Wilberforce Forum

THE BEGINNING: A SECOND LOOK AT THE FIRST SIN
"... a very readable and engaging discussion on the nature and consequences of the original sin using the biblical accounts as his primary authority."—*The American Journal of Biblical Theology*

SPEAKING CODE: UNRAVELING PAST BONDS TO REDEEM BROKEN CONVERSATIONS
"If you've ever longed for an effective tool to help replace hurtful speech or deadly silence with words that give life and heal hearts, *Speaking Code* is a must-read."—Kimberly Miller, author of *Boundaries for Your Soul*

GODLY CHARACTER(S): INSIGHTS FOR SPIRITUAL PASSION FROM THE LIVES OF 8 WOMEN IN THE BIBLE
"... these 'great eight' propel you towards habits of godliness—putting you in a place to receive grace and fall more deeply in love with your savior ..."
—Robert William Alexander, author of *The Gospel-Centered Life at Work*

REVEALED: A STORYBOOK BIBLE FOR GROWN-UPS
"*Revealed* sets out to crush any notion that the Bible is a safe, inspirational read. Instead the artwork here, historic and contemporary, takes a warts-and-all approach to even the most troubling passages, trading well-meaning elision for unvarnished truth."—J. Mark Bertrand, BibleDesignBlog.com

SQUAREHALOBOOKS.COM